It's A Faith Walk!

2 Corinthians 5:7. For we walk by faith, not by sight.

Habakkuk 2:3 Faith in God includes Faith in His timing.

Smith Wigglesworth

"There are two kinds of faith. There is the natural faith. But the supernatural faith is the gift of God."

"We become supernatural by the power of God. We find this power working through every part of our being "

Sheila Holm

It's A Faith Walk!
Copyright © 2014 Sheila Holm

All rights reserved.

No part of this book may be reproduced,
stored in a retrieval system or transmitted in any form
or by any means whether by electronic, mechanical,
photocopying, recording or any other,
except for brief quotations in printed reviews
without the prior written permission
from the author.

ISBN-10: 1495924556

ISBN-13: 978-1495924552

Unless otherwise indicated all scriptures are taken from the
New King James version of the Bible.

HISBest4us@aol.com

Printed in USA by HIS Best Publishing

Dedication, In Grateful Acknowledgment

To the memory of my Father (1918-2011) who did not lose faith in the midst of crisis and always taught us to do the right thing and my Mother who has taught by example, Irvin and Clarice, and to my California family, my cousins LaVonne and Gene McGee, and to our ancestors who emigrated to America for religious freedom and stood firm in faith.

To Bishop George Dallas McKinney for the depth of prophetic understanding required to merely lay his hands upon the back side of the draft manuscript, while it was merely an introductory letter God had me prepare before our 'meeting in three days,' for knowing the content and names (not included) before reading words, for being steadfast in helping me to keep on keepin' on, personally, encouraging me prior to and after each new adventure with God, while I remain grateful for your stand for all whom God sends to you!

To the memory (1918-2006) of Pastor Harald Bredesen; friendship developed during meetings with & introductions arranged by him, especially for setting up my interview with Benny Hinn. For sharing front row studio seats because God orchestrated my attendance as a witness of the prophetic word from Benny Hinn that God would send a Muslim man with a salvation testimony & his name would be Nasir (Dr. Nasir Siddiki).

To Pastor Steve Dittmar, Jubilee Church, and to my host families during my visits, especially to Michael and Wendy Blomquist and to the powerful testimony of Christina Thee to confirm the faith level of children at four years old, and to her family for providing the Tommy Tenney books, plus to the many prayer partners and the multiple blessings received by participating at Jubilee after each assignment 'in a new way' as orchestrated by God.

To Pastor Greg & Patricia Young, Collynn, Michelle & Jonathan, and adoption into the Young family.

To Pastor Earl Harrigan for being an amazing, anointed singer, especially **Walk on the Water** and **All Rise,** plus being a key witness to these days.

To Big John Hall for confirming God introduced us at a Rodney Howard-Browne meeting without sharing a word; God's plan when we were in each others' 'hometown.'

To John Willison for his mighty testimony and his offer to provide a tour of the TBN studio in Irving, Texas, a tour which has not happened, yet, however, it led to an introduction with the TBN producer, the opportunity to be interviewed on *Praise The Lord,* and for being the pilot who provided travel to a women's conference in Arkansas and to the Oklahoma church to encourage a pastor who was also from Nebraska.

To Ken Blanchard, for understanding exactly where my life was and what was required to get me out from under the rock to stand firm on the rock once again while living beyond the 'world plans' by diving 100% into Kingdom business!

To Rodney Howard-Browne for returning many times to San Diego at the exact time to renew the anointing that restores and prepares me to say YES for the next assignment.

To Pastors Sam & Rita Ankrah, Charles Benneh and their staff.

To Bishop Duncan Williams and to his worship team.

To singers Noel Robinson & Osene.

To pastors & Bishops in London, especially at Glory House, and to Bishop John Francis for sharing the gift of his *Finally* CD, for the amazing contributions made during my journey.

To the pastors, evangelists, teachers, and fellow prophets and apostles, and the leadership of the church, the speakers and saints participating in the various seminars and conferences around the world who have invited me, encouraged me, prayed with me and introduced me to host families who have become part of my breath of life gift from God.

To Kirk & Joni Bovill for their music.

To Apostle John Kelly and Pastor Harold Dewberry.

To the prayer partners, intercessors and prayer warriors walking the wall: Paul Davis, Carol Marfori, Lisa Hauri, Lib Jones, Gary & Cindy Graham and to the memory of 'Rozi' Graham Blegen (1953-2011), and Jan Franklin (December 7, 2008), and especially to Rebecca King, a deep women of God who realized the depth of my walk the moment we met because in our daily walk it all comes down to the truth about our lives in these days: *It's A Faith Walk!*

TABLE OF CONTENTS

	PAGE
Foreword by Bishop George Dallas McKinney	9
Prologue	13
1 What's a Faith Walk?	17
2 Faith In Action	27
3 The Whole Armor of God	35
4 Holy Spirit Guides Every Step	41
5 God Provides the Catapult	57
6 God's Assignments	65
7 Activation of Faith	73
8 God's Plans are Big	87
9 Jonah and the Whale	97
10 Is Your Answer Yes?	109
11 Launched to a Men's Ministry	119
12 Texas and Beyond in a Small Plane, Yikes!	133
13 Sent to the Other Side of the World: Down Under	149
14 Four Square Church, Aboriginal Cultural Center	161
15 God's Orchestration: Fiji and Kingdom of Tonga	173
16 A New Assignment Before I Was Unpacked	183
17 God Orchestrates A New Plan and Provision	191
18 In Search of Wigglesworth	203
19 Kingdom Business; Spiritual Warfare Conference	219
20 God's Orchestration to Become God's Witness	233
21 God fulfills a Lifetime Dream in Africa	243
Epilogue	259
A personal note 'just between us'	267
Footnotes	269
Books by Author	271
Acknowledgments	277
About the Author	287
Wigglesworth's Sermon: Dare To Believe, Then Command	289
America Founded upon Faith; Path to Freedom and Liberty	297

Freedom Monument: Wikipedia. National Monument to the Forefathers; Please view the DVD *Monumental* for further details. www.monumentalmovie.com. Kirk Cameron embarks upon the Pilgrim's journey from England to America. It will deepen your faith. Friends are buying DVD copies of *Monumental* for their family and friends.

Smith Wigglesworth *"There are two kinds of faith. There is the natural faith. But the supernatural faith is the gift of God. I cannot understand how God can give to any of His children glory and virtue, but it nevertheless is true that He does. There is something about believing in God that makes God willing to pass over a million people just to anoint you."*

Charles F. Parham *"The anointing of the Holy Spirit is given to illuminate His Word, to open the Scriptures, and to place the spiritual man in direct communication with the mind of God."*

Andrew Murray *"What now is faith? Nothing other than the certainty that what God says is true."*

Joni Eareckson Tada *"Faith isn't the ability to believe long and far into the misty future. It's simply taking God at His Word and taking the next step."*

Matthew Barnett *"Faith is believing that God is going to take you places before you even get there."*

William J. Seymour *"The Pentecostal power, when you sum it all up, is just more of God's love. If it does not bring more love, it is simply a counterfeit."*

Foreword

Sheila Holm has been on a 'Faith Walk' with God – 100% provision and 100% orchestration of all details – while she journeyed forth, church to church, business to business, government to government, and nation to nation, tribe to tribe, touching lives as part of God's master plan.

Sheila's journey of faith begins with the recognition that "we are totally and absolutely dependent upon God" and that God has predestined our lives for his purpose and provided a plan for us which supports his work on earth, prior to our birth.

Armed with this knowledge and faith, Sheila becomes a yielded vessel to be God's ambassador to encourage Christians, especially pastors, throughout America, Africa, Australia and Europe. Without sponsors or any visible means of support, she has traveled the world sustained by the faithfulness of God.

It's A Faith Walk confirms God's wisdom and plan within the testimony, "*God supplies all that we are and all that we need and He requests that we bring tithes of all that He gives us...*" based on the truth "*...the Earth is the Lords and the Fullness thereof,*" Psalms 24:1-2, I Corinthians 10:26 and 28.

Since God confirms he sends us forth, without an extra coin or tunic, to fulfill upon his purpose and plans for these days, Sheila was in the perfect position to go forth. She was without a corporate position (without finances), phone (communication), an auto (transportation), and credit cards or bank accounts (provision), so she was without other options, and yet, due to submitting to God's will and plans, she was sent around the globe, with God introducing her prior to her feet being on their soil and her testimony being expressed before the people while she was in their midst.

God's message through Sheila became a clear testimony to the people, *God's Storehouse Principle* is the message God shares through Sheila as she goes church to church, and it is uniting the body of Christ wherever God positions her feet around the globe ... because God's plans are big and God's heart is for all of the needs to be met, and for the people to be blessed, for his word is true, "*...ear has not heard, eye has not seen, and mind is not able to begin to conceive, the glory God has* ('in store') *prepared for those who love him.*"

God launched Sheila, filled her mouth so none can contradict God's plans, and he has expanded her territory and kept her from evil! And, as only God can do, he has humbled her with the fact the church needs more willing vessels, as God also caused a great revival that spread from England around the world through an illiterate man, Smith Wigglesworth. God sent Sheila on a journey to go to his church and the residence of his pastor. You will enjoy the unfolding of God's plans within **It's A Faith Walk,** especially because God confirmed all of the arrangements were made for Wigglesworth, also. He was guided 100% by the Holy Spirit and he went before planes, a phone, auto, bank debit and credit cards for God to use to arrange for his provision or travel.

You will be inspired when you read the words and realize the depth of planning and attention to detail our Lord will go to, to bless us, and to realize God has entrusted us with His property including all that we have been given, since birth: our life, time, treasure and talents. When you hear God's voice speaking to you about your *Faith Walk,* as you read the brief details shared in **It's A Faith Walk**

I pray you will be encouraged to take God's hand and go forward on your journey with our Lord, and then, become a participant in sharing your testimony with Sheila to spread God's truth around the world for the fellowship of believers is based upon **God's Storehouse Principle.**

Because God needs us to express our faith in this world more today than at any time in the history of our world, and when your faith walk is activated and **God's Storehouse Principle** is implemented, we will see what we have not seen, hear what we have not heard, and begin to conceive the glory God has ('in store') for us," and then, we will unite together, as one body, in one faith, and live in one accord, for each other, confirming *"**All of God's work done God's way will not lack God's supply.**"*

I strongly recommend **It's A Faith Walk** for it is a timely and urgent call to awaken the hearts of every Christian to grab God's hand and go forth on a *Faith Walk* with our Lord, and inspire and encourage fellow Faith Walkers so God's specific purpose predestined for you, to fulfill upon in your lifetime, shall be realized in your lifetime.

Bishop George Dallas McKinney

President, Pentecostal & Charismatic Churches North America (70,000+)

Board Member of Global Ministries: Billy Graham, Morris Cerullo, etc.

General Board Member, Church of God in Christ (COGIC)

Bishop and Pastor, St. Stephens Cathedral (COGIC)

Prologue

It's A Faith Walk is a journey God orchestrated after preparing me enough to get out of the whale exactly as Jonah found himself in so I could experience living in awe and wonder each step of the way. Since God started with a card-carrying, pew-warming, protestant denominational gal, there was a lot of preparation which needed to take place! God's training prior to being sent did not stop when God orchestrated travel since I was sent 'without an extra coin or tunic' and God arranged personal introductions before I arrived and confirmed plans after I showed up, plus, there was a lot of 'on the job training' and 'filling me as an empty vessel' with exact words precisely when they were needed.

Like many who have asked me, I wanted to see the signs, wonders and miracles. I did not realize it was my limited human understanding which was blocking the experience! Before the journey, my prayer requests were merely words about what I want God to do. Sad, but I was focused upon exactly what and how I expected God to proceed, to 'get it done and also do it all for me.' I never saw my prayers from God's perspective. As soon as I did, everything I had prayed up to that point sounded lame.

Not an easy realization to comprehend.

God had to show me that we do not know his word or that His promises are true, so we are not able to begin to comprehend the glorious things God has 'in store for us.'

We have a very limited, human view of our life. I pray that changes for God has a God sized view of our life. His plans for us are big. It is painful to hear so many people state the church, the body of Christ, is still in the pre-toddler phase and not walking yet, only hoping to hear a good word on Sunday that will carry the people through the week. I trust this is why God has shown me how much he has planned for us and why we need to operate as bible based and spirit-filled believers. The first time I heard that, I did not know the difference between the churches. Without God's guidance, we lack the ability to comprehend or act on God's plan for our life. I pray you will lean on God's word and the guidance of the Holy Spirit and not on your own understanding.

A dear man of God told me that he asked God to show him **"*Who is this woman?*"** God's vision of me showed the man how the mouse is to the elephant (confirmed as the body of Christ). He said I was so persistent, shouting for the elephant to move. but I was ignored. Plus, during all attempts while I was biting on the back ankles, swinging on the tail and shouting, **"*Move,*"** and even as I ran to the left ear, bit the ear and shouted. But, I would not stop there. I ran to the right ear, bit the ear many times and shouted until the elephant took the first step.

God showed him my effort caused the body to move. I was encouraged, especially since I have met with many leaders in the body and I've shared God's deep concerns about the body not being equipped and trained so we can grow to maturity. & flow together.

After all, we are to be wise as serpents & gentle as doves.

That combination takes a LOT of practice!

We were not to participate with the world / enemy, merely to know what they are doing. God has been clear, we need to be equipped and trained to faith walk as an Ambassador of our Lord and Savior Jesus Christ!

Example of becoming weak in our efforts: Check with **spell check.** It only recognizes demonizing or demonized not discipling or discipled.

As fellow members of the body of Christ, we have a lot of work to do!

May the words I share based upon all God has shown to me, bless and encourage you to go on a faith walk with God walking in power and authority, utilizing your gifts, talents, skills and abilities to bless the people God directs you to or places in your path. Then, share your testimony with me and all in the world who have ears to hear.

Until I hear the details about your faith walk, I pray you will continue to experience HIS Best!

Sheila

2 Corinthians 5:7. For we walk by faith, not by sight

Joni Eareckson Tada *"Faith isn't the ability to believe long and far into the misty future. It's simply taking God at His Word and taking the next step."*

Romans 1:17 For in it the righteousness of God is revealed from faith to faith; as it is written, *"The just shall live by faith."*

Kathryn Kuhlman *"Beloved, the secret of victory over fear is very simple - it is trusting Jesus! One of the most frequent expressions on His lips throughout His life here on earth was, "Fear not!" So look up! Faith in God has in times past "subdued kingdoms, wrought righteousness, obtained promises, stopped the mouths of lions, quenched the violence of fire, escaped the edge of the sword...turned to flight the armies of the aliens"* **(Hebrews 11:33, 34)** *and FAITH CAN DO IT AGAIN! You are not only a conqueror, you can be more than a conqueror through Him Who loves you!"*

Galatians 6:10. Therefore, as we have opportunity, let us do good to all, especially to those who are of the household of faith.

John G Lake *"Take the shackles off God. Let Him have a chance to bless mankind without ecclesiastical limitations."*

Chapter 1   What's A Faith Walk?

God's desire is to be on a faith walk with us each second of every day.

What? This was new news to me! I've been 'in the church' for decades (no need at this point to reveal the exact number of decades) and yet, I was never aware of the process or prepared to embark upon an adventure with God. However, it is true that God is faithful and proved it, moment by moment, for this journey has been exciting and inspiring. At times, so powerful in the moment that I have to go back and look at my journal to realize the depth of God's orchestration to get me from point A to point B.

Now I realize why we are not seeing and hearing of the miracles on a regular basis. We are not speaking about the blessings when we gather together and fellowship with each other.

We are not sharing the glorious things God does for us because He loves us.

A faith walk is not about the global travel, the sights and opportunities which God arranged for me, it is about the submission to God to be guided by the Holy Spirit so His purpose and plan for our life can be fulfilled while we are on earth, praying as Jesus taught us to pray that it shall be 'on earth as it is in heaven'.

In the Beginning

It's A Faith Walk! is based upon a true story, my story about God's wake-up call to me, a process which was not included during years of being in church. Plus, I'm including a few details of the travels God arranged during a few months of my journey.

It is an honor for me to share a few of the details within about seven months of travel with God because you can tell I was asleep at the wheel of my life and it is clear that all of the credit goes to God. As I have told host families, **"*All I have to do is show up*** (empty vessel) ***and be willing to serve*** (let God fill me to overflowing, to share His word with the people)."

It did not happen overnight. God had to start at zero. No discipleship training; thought I was accomplished but it was 'in the world'! The world had not 'been nice'. Long story short, I was forced on to multiple social security and driver's license numbers after bringing the injustices within the justice system to light.

Judges and an attorney served prison terms due to being sentenced on Federal RICO charges. Each time the numbers supposedly had to change for my protection, the agents/agencies used dire consequences language: *"If you do not change your number(s), we cannot protect you."* Then, as soon as I proceeded, they said, *"If you let anything merge with your prior number(s), we cannot protect you."* What? How does a citizen re-create a life without a work or credit history?

After following all of the instructions of the agents and agency policies, and losing ground in my life for two decades, I found out their statements were lies! I never had a clear, separate record as my record. Their lies resulted in all details being merged into one big mess the entire time, so, all of the costs/damages, and impact upon every aspect of my life were for naught!

Each time I brought the truth to the agents, they offered help but, they never took a step to clear up the mess. Instead, after I proved their lies they stated I have no file on record. My record was removed from the system which was their attempt to cover up their errors, but it erased me. To the world, there was no record to confirm I even existed. But, God has my full record!

Clearly, I thought I was 100% right when I told God I could do nothing. I was down for the count. I trusted I was done! I had no sources or resources to tap and no way to start my life over again. I had lost perspective. I forgot that God knew all of the 'behind the scenes' details long before I knew anything sinister was going on. I was well educated. I followed all of their instructions. I thought I knew the score!

Since all of the expenses and effort extended were for naught, 100% wasted, down the drain, I did not re-establish my life. I did not arrange for another auto, I did not obtain a new phone number, a bank / debit or credit account. I was being specific when I told God that I could do nothing! After all, what could I do when I did not have a way to establish communication, transportation or do anything which required financial support or purchase anything, especially flight tickets, payment for hotel rooms, etc. to travel.

Problem: I was thinking in my own mind, aka, small, limited, human capacity.

So, it was a wake-up call for me when God took my hand, because I was truly in a fetal position on the floor. I had nothing I felt God could use. I told God I was done, and I repeatedly reminded God I could do nothing. But, God in His soft and gentle voice through the Holy Spirit confirmed the plan, ***"Through Me you can do all things."***

Matthew 19:26. Jesus looked at *them* and said to them, ***"With men this is impossible, but with God all things are possible."***

Powerful and endearing, but, I did not jump up, get on task or proceed, yet.

I grew up in the church. I believed in God and God knew I trusted Him and wanted to proceed based only upon His wisdom, but I had no map to follow. I prayed regularly and therefore I felt I sought God's counsel. However, even though I was raised in the church and confirmed on Pentecost Sunday, the annual tradition in the Lutheran church, on purpose, the people are not sure if they are truly saved. Many still ask me. They do not know how to be delivered and set free from the enemy. They do not know how to distinguish God's voice from the closest counterfeit, Satan or his minions. There were no instructions regarding how to become spirit-filled Christians so we can operate in power and authority. I had not heard of the term 'Holy Spirit in-filling' so I had no idea how to make the request.

Proverbs 3:4-6. *And* so find favor and high esteem in the sight of God and man. [5] Trust in the Lord with all your heart, And lean not on your own understanding; [6] In all your ways acknowledge Him, And He shall direct your paths.

Without the Holy Spirit, I had gone forward in life without a road map! What I had learned was how to live per a 'success plan' of being in a church, plus attending and obtaining a Christian college education, and it actually caused me to lean nearly 99+% on my own (man's / woman's / world's) understanding.

I thought I had a great plan. My family sacrificed so I could be trained and heavily educated to know the ways of the world to become successful. So that is exactly what I did. I reached a point where some even called me wealthy. Some thought I had captured the brass ring.

However, in Kingdom business I was not considered rich. I did not recognize any distinctions between the plans revealed during my years (decades) of education and how the plans were a direct conflict to God's plan for my life, yet, until all of the plans crumbled, aka everything in my world fell apart. I did not realize the plan of the enemy. I had no knowledge of what the devil could do to us in his effort to lie and deceive, plus steal, kill and destroy.

The enemy's plan can take on the appearance of being a grand plan, while it often becomes 100% self-directed and takes on the names of greed, jealousy, envy or lust for power, but the results are all about the same: *The world plan can crumble everything in our life within moments because the world plan is not built upon the rock.*

Simple concept, but, it was not 'taught'.

Seriously, stating I was in a fetal position on the floor when God took my hand is mildly stating I had hit bottom or I passed bottom on the way to falling into the abyss.

The details are not as important right now (they are the focus of a separate book on God's Storehouse Principle, God's plan for our lives vs the world based plan / system) as understanding the differences in the concept of discipling each other to be successful, either: 1. in this world, or 2. in Kingdom (being about our Father's) business. We are focused on one. We just need to be sure it's the right one! The two paths are available and God gives us 'free will' to choose our path, so I hope we will help each other and disciple people in the truth so we know which path we are choosing with each decision we make.

**God took my hand
when I surrendered & cried out to Him!**

I was so lost, I told God I needed vision to confirm what He wanted me to do and I would do that.

During the night, God showed me three visions.

First one: I was surrounded by all of my 'projects,' courses I taught at the University for a new Management Certificate Program, conference speaking topics, Entrepreneurial course materials for the US Federal contracts, etc., topics on top confirmed the stacks were representative of the entire accomplishments in my life to date, so there were stacks of paper everywhere. In that moment, a large funnel appeared. I was staring at the bottom of the funnel to see exactly what God was going to show me, as God scooped up all of the papers and inserted them into the funnel. But, as soon as the funnel was filled with all of my stuff God merely tapped the small end of the funnel and all of the papers fell in all directions. As I watched them flying through the air I realized no specific task was being identified and I did not even realize God put His hand through the small end of the funnel until I saw God pull me through. It was a shock to watch the movie of my life with God picking me up. All God had in His hand was me. I was so human in that moment, plus I was confused because not one topic appeared amongst the papers so I asked, *"What do you want from me?"* And the Holy Spirit softly confirmed when I saw God's hand lift me up higher in the air, *"What I want is you."*

It was a humbling experience. I had no idea what God could do with me. I was in tears as God showed me the second vision. I was on a platform with the floodlights on the stage shining bright. God made it a familiar experience as it was exactly what I experience as a conference speaker. It was exciting because I recognized all of the people in the first row. God said, *"You are here for them."* I told God it was not very much to fill my life, by being here for the people I already know. As I said this, God turned the floodlights on the multitude which stretched out across the land in all directions. I immediately confirmed I did not know any of these people as God stated, *"Because you blessed the ones you know, they blessed the rest."*

I was embarrassed. To me, this sounded rather lofty. God knew my concern and showed me the third vision. God turned the view to show my side profile so I could see my words leaving my lips and going out to the front row and then bouncing throughout the multitude.

I was in awe as God showed me how His words leaving my mouth and traveling to the heart of the first person and on to the next and the next, on and on until they reached the multitude.

It appeared the same to me as a stone does when it is cast upon the water and it touches the water many times while it skips across a lake. God knew I used to try and make stones skip across the water with cousins when I was young so God used that analogy and it made sense to me.

However, I still felt I was incapable of being a representative for God, an Ambassador for Christ.

John G. Lake "*Do you know what prayer is? It is not begging God for this and that. The first thing we have to do is to get you beggars to quit begging until a little faith moves in your souls.*"

1 Corinthians 2:4-5. And my speech and my preaching were not with persuasive words of human wisdom, but in demonstration of the Spirit and of power, [5] that your faith should not be in the wisdom of men but in the power of God.

Rick Renner "*Faith is the spark that ignites the impossible and causes it to become possible. When a person's faith is activated, it sets in motion supernatural power that enables that person to do what he normally would never be able to do!*"

Benny Hinn "*I walk in the realm of the supernatural.*"

Chapter 2 Faith In Action

Journey Without An Extra Coin Or Tunic

A faith walk is truly the result of letting God orchestrate our life, God's plan for us which is beyond our human comprehension.

God predestined great things for us before we arrived on Earth! We may use our free choice and free will to never embark on the plans God has 'in store' for us, while I pray you will seek to embark on a journey with God for you will be blessed.

In the meantime, may you be blessed by the details and the masterful orchestration God arranged on my behalf as I traveled with him church to church, business to business, and nation to nation.

It was all done without an extra coin or tunic.

Matthew 10:9 "Do not take gold or silver or copper in your belts (purse); take no bag for the journey, or extra tunic…for the worker is worth his keep."

In fact, I heard a story, a testimony about **God's Storehouse Principle.** It is the focus and title of a separate book, a journey with God which has given me insights into what has happened to the body of Christ and God caused the message to become the content and then the repeated them when He arranged for me to preach in churches / businesses, and to the nations.

Back to the man's story: It starts when he was taken to heaven during his surgery. God showed him a huge warehouse. When they entered, the man saw miles of gifts, all wrapped in white glossy paper and tied with beautiful red bows.

The packages were stacked neatly and identified with our names on each tag. God directed the man to his specific stack. It was so high the man could not see the top of the stack. He was in shock.

God explained that most of the gifts we possess since birth, our talents and abilities which would help others, the blessings God has prepared for us to receive and to share, often remain in the stack during our lifetime as we do not understand the process of what we are to do when two or more gather together for Christ is the midst when we are fellowshipping with each other. We are to be about Kingdom business, our Father's business, as Christ was, sharing the blessings we are and all that we have with each other so none shall leave the assembly in lack.

Pew warming, seeking a good word should not be enough for us, for Christ resides in our heart and we are to operate in power and authority so all shall be blessed and none leave the gathering in lack.

God confirmed some believers only believe part of the truth and portions of God's word. Many believe Pentecost happened. Many believe key parts of God's word or most of it. However, there are many who do not believe the Holy Spirit guides us or that we are empowered by the Holy Spirit to walk in power and authority so we can do all God has need of us to do while we are on earth. Jesus taught to us pray so it shall be **"On earth as it is in heaven…"**

When we are not walking in the power and authority of the Holy Spirit we can mess up so much and miss God. We will proced without realizing how to proceed. Only God will replace, restore and bless beyond all that we can pray for or do when He guides us through the His Spirit to be in action for each other so God's work will be done **on earth as it is in heaven**.

White boxes with red bows. Gifts unopened and people in need. A visual which sticks in my mind. It shifted my thinking because I finally realized I cannot out do God. When I heard this, I remembered people quoting God is a BIG God and wants to bless, but, in all of my years in church I was not seeing the blessings flow as the Doxology states: "…*from whom all blessings flow…*"

I dismissed the thought since I had experienced some devastating, life-altering circumstances. They were so severe they separated me from people in the church because they said bad things do not happen to good people, aka *"You must have done something to upset God."*

The negative experiences and the negative people in the church both rendered me speechless. When I called a dear prayer partner, she told me, *"If you could run into the street and throw out your top three problems, would you do it?"* The answer took no time to calculate for it would be great to be able to merely throw away my problems. But then, she said, *"Now, since all of your neighbors had the same offer and they did the same thing, which ones would you run out and pick up if you knew everybody was going to run out and pick up three?"*

Wow, I was shocked. That did not take time to calculate, either, since I am comfortable with the problems I am dealing with. However, she then said, *"Why are you holding on to any problems? Do you believe God will guide you through any problem you might experience or not?"*

I was absolutely used to carrying everything tight, holding on to everything. I wondered if perhaps I was stuck in my own mess? Then I heard the cliche comment: *"Let go and Let God!"* It was simple. It was specific. It was a wake-up call!

Journey as An Empty Vessel

I trust it will not be as difficult for you as it was for me to become an 'empty vessel' so God could fill me with His word, His wisdom for the situation exactly in the moment when it is needed.

It makes me think about the study I did in genealogy to trace our family lines back to Norway, England and Scotland. Our English ancestors were Church of England (Episcopalian), Scottish relatives were Church of Scotland (Presbyterian), and Norwegian relatives were Scandinavian Lutheran. In the Scotland to Canada to America research, I found an obituary of a great-great aunt whose husband stated she was many wonderful things and then he added she was his best friend 'of Quaker ancestors.' This was a shock!

They came to America for religious and financial freedom. I learned about the separation of church and state from them, as they did not want a Church of America!

Since nothing in the family bibles indicated a relative was linked to Quakers, I called to talk to my Mom. Dad answered the call and set the record straight with his response, ***"There's nobody in your Mom's family quiet enough to be a Quaker!"***

As you can tell from my Dad's confirmation, God had a lot to do to help me completely empty this vessel for God to be able to fill me to overflowing. It's the more of God / Holy Spirit and less of me / flesh process. It is a blessing because you only want God's truth and wisdom to be expressed to the people. It is critical to seek the Lord's training and the Holy Spirit's infilling so we can proceed with the step-by-step guidance as you will see when you read the adventurous day when witches danced & attempted to poison me in Africa; night when a voodoo princess (God protected me because she was a priestess) tried to curse me off the planet during a Spiritual Warfare Conference in Earl's Court, London!

When empty and fully submitted, God can do mighty things and all that is needed will be provided.

Remember the little insignificant detail about not having a phone (auto or accounts) in America? Well a man from New Zealand doing business in London, the same man God prompted to buy my round trip ticket from London so I would have a way home found this status to be unacceptable. He said, *I need to be able to call you and FAX information to you so when you return to America set up two phone lines.*

Again, I told him it was not possible. He ignored me and said, *If you have to set them up in my name and if the phone company wants to check on my record, you can tell them I am with AT&T.*

This seemed impossible.

When I called the top manager of the local phone company she said I would not be able to have phone lines due to the multiple social security numbers issued to me.

I called the phone company back. This time, I confirmed the man's details about being a citizen of New Zealand, working in England and needing two lines.

The employee did not ask if the man had a record with AT&T, she only wanted to know his social security number. When I reminded her he was born in New Zealand so he does not have a social security number, without hesitation she said, *"Ah, that's right. Does he want a morning or afternoon appointment tomorrow?"*

As a citizen, the wait would be about ten days to two weeks. However, without knowing anything about the man or that he even exists, the phone lines were established the next day. It has been impossible to change the lines back to my name, even though I am the one paying the monthly bills, so 'on paper' the two phone lines had to remain in his name.

Faith Made Evident

When God arranged for me to be in Ghana, West Africa, I attended a church service with Pastor Sam Ankrah due to God orchestrating a ride from the hotel with a man who did not know me, yet, Pastor Charles Benneh. God told me the exact moment when I was to go to the lobby, and then, God told me to ask a specific man if he was going to church; the question led to a friendship which included attendance at his ordination in London, England several years later, with the opportunity to meet his wife and family, and our friendship continues to this day.

God showed me so much within minutes. I was amazed and in awe of the faith expressed by the people.

It was in early August. The heat and humidity were both about 100. The men were in long sleeve shirts and ties, holding white kerchiefs while dancing and praising the Lord.

Their faces were radiant. Their smiles were contagious.

This was a new type of 'church experience,' clearly not 'an American church experience'.

I've not seen men dancing as though nobody is watching and praising, let alone doing it in the extreme hot temperature with high humidity.

I asked Pastor Sam and he said, *"They are like you. They live by faith, but, it is different for the people here because they have to pay at least $200/month in rent alone and most of the people do not earn $200/month. Their testimonies are strong for you see they have to depend upon God's provision in their life every day of their life."*

I felt I was filled with faith and I knew my life was spirit filled, while the training program with God is like 'on the job training' as we continue hand in hand with Him during our Faith Walk!

Kenneth Copeland – *"God's plan for your life is bigger than everything coming against it."*

Hebrews 11: 1. Now faith is the substance of things hoped for, the evidence of things not seen.

Philippians 4:19-20. And my God shall supply all your need according to His riches in glory by Christ Jesus. [20] Now to our God and Father be glory forever and ever. Amen.

Chapter 3 The Whole Armor of God

The Whole Armor of God

Ephesians 6:10-20. Finally, my brethren, be strong in the Lord and in the power of His might. [11] Put on the whole armor of God that you may be able to stand against the wiles of the devil. [12] For we do not wrestle against flesh and blood, but against principalities, against powers, against the rulers of the darkness of this age, against spiritual *hosts* of wickedness in the heavenly *places.* [13] Therefore take up the whole armor of God, that you may be able to withstand in the evil day, and having done all, to stand.

[14] Stand therefore, having girded your waist with truth, having put on the breastplate of righteousness, [15] and having shod your feet with the preparation of the gospel of peace; [16] above all, taking the shield of faith with which you will be able to quench all the fiery darts of the wicked one. [17] And take the helmet of salvation, and the sword of the Spirit, which is the word of God; [18] praying always with all prayer and supplication in the Spirit, being watchful to this end with all perseverance and supplication for all the saints

[19] and for me, that utterance may be given to me, that I may open my mouth boldly to make known the mystery of the gospel, [20] for which I am an ambassador ...

Hebrews 4:12 For the word of God [is] quick, and powerful, and sharper than any two edged sword, piercing even to the dividing asunder of soul and spirit, and of the joints and marrow, and [is] a discerner of the thoughts and intents of the heart.

Grateful for the opportunities to pray together and review the scriptures about how Satan is the closest counterfeit, and stressing that we need to be as wise as the serpent (Satan) and yet, remain as gentle as doves!

Matthew 10:16. *"Behold, I send you out as sheep in the midst of wolves. Therefore be wise as serpents and harmless as doves..."*

However, it usually follows the moments when 'they are trying to kill one of God's servants' and it is a bit disconcerting and then humbling because it is me! I can confirm God will give us the exact words as we need them, for us to be victorious in the battle!

Again, as you will see, God has raised me up from being able to do nothing to being able to wield the sword in mighty battles in which many hear the depth of God's wisdom and desire to surrender fully to him.

God handles the moments...I merely have to show up empty and let God fill me!

Matthew 10:19. *"...do not worry about how or what you should speak. For it will be given to you in that hour what you* *should speak;* [20] *for it is not you who speak, but the Spirit of your Father who speaks in you…"*

God Strengthens Us,

When We Are Weak God Makes Us Strong

2 Corinthians 12: 9-12. … *"My grace is sufficient for you, for My strength is made perfect in weakness."* Therefore most gladly I will rather boast in my infirmities, that the power of Christ may rest upon me. [10] Therefore I take pleasure in infirmities, in reproaches, in needs, in persecutions, in distresses, for Christ's sake. For when I am weak, then I am strong.

2 Corinthians 13: 7-14. Now I pray to God that you do no evil, not that we should appear approved, but that you should do what is honorable, though we may seem disqualified. [8] For we can do nothing against the truth, but for the truth. [9] For we are glad when we are weak and you are strong. And this also we pray, that you may be made complete. [10] Therefore I write these things being absent, lest being present I should use sharpness, according to the authority which the Lord has given me for edification and not for destruction.

Greetings and Benediction: [11] Finally, brethren, farewell. Become complete. Be of good comfort, be of one mind, live in peace; and the God of love and peace will be with you. [12] Greet one another with a holy kiss. [13] All the saints greet you. [14] The grace of the Lord Jesus Christ, and the love of God, and the communion of the Holy Spirit *be* with you all. Amen.

If You Can Use Anyone Lord, You Can Use Me

In my travels, I've met Joni Bovill, a former worship team member with Ron Kenoly. Her voice and songs have blessed me as have Ron's songs, especially this CD and song title, ***Majesty.***

So, what did God do next?

God immediately provided options for me to embark upon assignments, journey after journey masterfully orchestrating everything for me: introductions, invitations, connections, transportation housing and travel, while the world would have left me in the fetal position on the floor because the world had destroyed me and provided no answers or options.

Later, God sent me on a *'Search for Wigglesworth'* (Chapter 18) and after the journey I was so excited to expound upon the glorious things God did for and through Wigglesworth when God stopped me and put our faith walk journey into perspective: "*I am the same yesterday, today and tomorrow. What I did for and through Wigglesworth, I am doing the same for you.*"

God's message was so clear and simple that it stopped me in my tracks. God did it all for me and God still had to remind me: **Wigglesworth did not have a phone, an auto, a debit or credit card, either.** God keeps the message so simple!

Praying these words are speaking deeply to you, because I want God's best for you and all in your family & lineage on to the 3rd and 4th generation. I have no reason to merely share the glorious things God has done for me without confirming upon your heart that God loves you so much He wants to be on a faith walk with you, also!

The testimony of our life is glorious when God is in control. Many say, "***Let go and let God***" while they may or may not be connected with the one true God, the trinity of God the Father, Son and Holy Spirit. Some churches (perhaps most churches, since the denominational churches have become based upon man's traditions and beliefs, following a man's understanding when the bible is clear: *Do not lean upon man's understanding;* the churches actually want followers of Christ to only believe what they believe based upon a man's interpretation) only want to believe part of the bible and many churches dismiss the Holy Spirit even though God confirmed the truth through the prophets and Jesus Christ.

It is critical for us to declare who our Lord is and for us to be willing to declare from our rooftops (they did not have radios, TV or internet in those days) as the prophets and apostles describe the sharing of testimony of what God does for each of us because His love for us is so inspiring and encouraging. Casting Crowns songs: **Until the Whole World Hears, Praise You In The Storm, Courageous, Voice of Truth and Who Am I,** etc.

Each time I hear a testimony, tears flow! There are some testimonies shared through You Tube videos which are so special, I have to listen a few times because I cannot control the tears so I can see the video the first or even the second time. The tears are not 100% due to the details, because if we merely hear it as though it happened for someone else then we are missing the key point: **God's orchestration.** God wants the results of our faith walk to be our testimony. It is God's desire that we share our faith one to another whenever we gather together for we confirm to each other what God is doing in our lives. Is God's peace evident?

Philippians 4:13. I can do all things through Christ who strengthens me.

I will never forget a unique experience with a driver in London. We were definitely proceeding at high speed. I was asked about my life in America. I started to share a few details about having to deal with the debacle caused by the agents when she exited the M-25 without decreasing speed before she slammed on the brakes and brought the car to a complete halt. She had one question which she stated with great intensity: *"Do We Serve The Same God?"*

There was a moment of silence. I wanted to say of course we do. It was a wow, sit up and take notice of the words which are spilling out of my mouth moment.

With our words, we either confirm Christ resides in our heart or the world has been able to influence our thoughts and allowed the enemy to enter into our conversation. I stand in awe of God's wisdom being shared through me & I pray it is evident in my life!

I've learned that to be an Ambassador of Christ, people should be able to copy anything I say and do. At first, this thought was mind-numbing. However, the difference in how our life unfolds is amazing. ***Lord help us be mindful of our words so Your words will be heard in our conversations for your words can change a life in a split second!***

Charles F. Parham *"The anointing of the Holy Spirit is given to illuminate His Word, to open the Scriptures, and to place the spiritual man in direct communication with the mind of God."*

Chapter 4   Holy Spirit Guides Every Step

What Jesus promised is true.

John 14:26 But the Helper, the Holy Spirit, whom the Father will send in My name, He will teach you all things, and bring to your remembrance all things that I said to you.

Acts 2:1 [Coming of the Holy Spirit] When the Day of Pentecost had fully come, they were all with one accord in one place.

Acts 2:4 And they were all filled with the Holy Spirit and began to speak with other tongues, as the Spirit gave them utterance.

Peter's Sermon begins at 14: But Peter, standing up with the eleven, raised his voice and said to them, "Men of Judea and all who dwell in Jerusalem, let this be known to you, and heed my words. [15] For these are not drunk, as you suppose, since it is *only* the third hour of the day. [16] But this is what was spoken by the prophet Joel: [17] 'And it shall come to pass in the last days, says God, that I will pour out of My Spirit on all flesh; Your sons and your daughters shall prophesy, your young men shall see visions, your old men shall dream dreams. [18] And on My menservants and on My maidservants I will pour out My Spirit in those days; and they shall prophesy.

Acts 2:33 Therefore being exalted to the right hand of God, and having received from the Father the promise of the Holy Spirit, He poured out this which you now see and hear.

Acts 2:38 Then Peter said to them, "Repent, and let every one of you be baptized in the name of Jesus Christ for the remission of sins; and you shall receive the gift of the Holy Spirit.

Romans 8:26+ Likewise the Spirit also helps in our weaknesses. For we do not know what we should pray for as we ought, but the Spirit Himself makes intercession for us with groanings which cannot be uttered. [27] Now He who searches the hearts knows what the mind of the Spirit *is,* because He makes intercession for the saints according to *the will of* God. [28] And we know that all things work together for good to those who love God, to those who are the called according to *His* purpose. [29] For whom He foreknew, He also predestined *to be* conformed to the image of His Son, that He might be the firstborn among many brethren. [30] Moreover whom He predestined, these He also called; whom He called, these He also justified; and whom He justified, these He also glorified.[31] What then shall we say to these things? If God *is* for us, who *can be* against us?

How does God guide us by the Holy Spirit?

John the Baptist proclaimed:

Matthew 3:11 I indeed baptize you with water unto repentance, but He who is coming after me is mightier than I, whose sandals I am not worthy to carry. He will baptize you with the Holy Spirit and fire.

As followers of Christ we were warned:

Matthew 12:32 Anyone who speaks a word against the Son of Man, it will be forgiven him; but whoever speaks against the Holy

Spirit, it will not be forgiven him, either in this age or in the age to come.

The commission to all:

Matthew 28:19 Go therefore and make disciples of all the nations, baptizing them in the name of the Father and of the Son and of the Holy Spirit

We do not have to be concerned about the 'assignment':

Luke 12:12 For the Holy Spirit will teach you in that very hour what you ought to say."

A good example of what is referred to as Holy Spirit in-filling is the night when God prompted Mary Boddy, the wife of Smith Wigglesworth's Pastor Alex Boddy, to lay hands upon Wigglesworth and pray with him for the Holy Spirit to fill him.

Wigglesworth was saved. However, he was not walking in power and authority.

In the scriptures, it was the same for Saul before he became Paul. God showed Saul the vision while Saul was on the road. Then, God prompted Ananias to go and visit Saul. Ananias knew Saul's past so he was very resistant to accept the assignment, but, God instructed Ananias to pray with Saul that he may receive his sight and be filled with the Holy Spirit.

Acts 9:17 And Ananias went his way and entered the house; and laying his hands on him he said, *"Brother Saul, the Lord Jesus, who appeared to you on the road as you came, has sent me that you may receive your sight and be filled with the Holy Spirit."*

When filled with the Holy Spirit, God can and will provide the wisdom and word of knowledge directly to you in the exact moment when it is required. When Wigglesworth proceeded through the long prayer lines, God was able to give him the specific instructions for each person. I remember hearing about a man being punched in the stomach. The people were stunned to see Wigglesworth wind up his arm as a mighty baseball pitcher on the mound in order to gain the momentum required to deliver the punch. What did God do with the intensity of the blow to the exact spot of the man's stomach cancer tumor? The tumor was destroyed. If Wigglesworth did not have the ability to hear the message direct from God, he would not have known to wind up his arm and deliver the blow in the exact spot necessary for the man to be healed.

This being said, we the people need to have faith for the healing is a two pronged process. God's healing power coupled with our faith.

I remember hearing about a person entering Wigglesworth's prayer line a second time. Wigglesworth dismissed the man. The man was very upset, but, Wigglesworth sternly told the man he was already prayed for but he was filled with unbelief. A brief quote from Wigglesworth's 1919 sermon **Dare to Believe, Then Command.**[1] Complete sermon begins on page 309.

"He that believeth on Me!" What is this? What does it mean? How can just believing bring these things to pass? What virtue is there in it? There is virtue in these words because He declares

them. If we will receive this word and declare it, the greater works shall be accomplished. This is a positive declaration of His, "He that believeth on Me, greater works than these shall he do," <u>but unbelief has hindered our progress in the realm of the spiritual</u>.

<u>Put away unbelief.</u> Open your heart to God's grace. Then God will come in and place in you a definite faith. He wants to remove every obstruction that is in the world before you. By His grace He will enable you to be so established in His truth, so strong in the Lord and in the power of His might, that whatever comes across your path to obstruct you, you can arise in divine power and rebuke and destroy it.

Paul explains the difference between the baptism of repentance conducted by John the Baptist which confirmed salvation through our Savior and Lord Jesus Christ and the baptism in the Holy Spirit when he met with some (12) of the disciples in Ephesus:

Acts 19:1-7. And it happened, while Apollos was at Corinth, that Paul, having passed through the upper regions, came to Ephesus. And finding some disciples ² he said to them, "*Did you receive the Holy Spirit when you believed?*"

So they said to him, "*We have not so much as heard whether there is a Holy Spirit.*" ³ And he said to them, "*Into what then were you baptized?*" So they said, "*Into John's baptism.*"

⁴ Then Paul said, "*John indeed baptized with a baptism of repentance, saying to the people that they should believe on Him who would come after him, that is, on Christ Jesus.*"

⁵ When they heard *this*, they were baptized in the name of the Lord Jesus. ⁶ And <u>when Paul had laid hands on them, the Holy Spirit came upon them, and they spoke with tongues and prophesied</u>. ⁷ Now the men were about twelve in all.

So, God is consistent throughout His word and when He prompts the Holy Spirit to speak to the hearts of those who are willing to act on faith in obedience to God's promptings:

1. Ananias was sent by God to lay hands on and fill Saul / Paul with the Holy Spirit.

2. Paul met with some of the disciples in Ephesus and taught them about both baptisms: a. in the name of our Lord Jesus Christ, the baptism of repentance, and b. of the Holy Spirit. Paul then laid hands on the believers and they were filled with the Holy Spirit and they spoke in tongues and prophesied. It was the same prompting by God when

3. Mary Boddy, wife of Pastor Alexander Boddy, laid hands on Smith Wigglesworth a man who was already baptized and knew Christ as his Savior, and he was immediately filled with the Holy Spirit.

4. Wigglesworth then traveled the globe and the gifts of the Holy Spirit were evident: a) many were healed, and b) filled with the Holy Spirit, nation to nation.

Being Understood by the People, in their Language

Twice in America God surpassed the interpreter during meetings with Hispanic congregations.

It was not me sharing a dialect they could comprehend even though seven years of Spanish classes were on my resume. My Spanish is a very unique blend of the basics and only accessible to insert as a response if someone has a lot of patience and they are speaking very, very slowly to give me time to prepare a phrase.

God anointed both meetings. All in attendance were being empowered by the Holy Spirit. I thought I was doing well with the message when I realized the translators were not able to continue as they went into the gift of laughter with the people.

In one of the Hispanic meetings, two women were very concerned. They were not aware of what was going on as they had not experienced the power of the Holy Spirit before. They stood up, wobbled the best they could until they reached the side wall. I grabbed the microphone off the stand and walked toward them to see if they were OK. As soon as I was within six rows, they went down sideways under the power of the Holy Spirit, landing on their sides as they gently slid down along the wall.

Later, both translators told me they knew what I was saying since I was speaking Spanish. They laughed as they thanked God they did not have to continue translating. This was odd to me. Clearly, I was hearing English being spoken so it did not make sense until the second translator stated the same fact and the people confirmed the truth.

God was speaking through me so the people would hear His message in their own dialect of the Spanish language.

This also happened in the Kingdom of Tonga. The Minister of Finance opened the meeting with an intense introduction in Tongan. The only words I understood when he spoke were

America and my name. The men had no expression on their faces. They know some English. However, I did not have a translator. After the meeting they confirmed God gave them a deep message. Each message was unique to each person and they knew it was direct from God. God did this for them merely because I was willing to speak. I am in awe of all our God does because He loves us.

Acts 2:1-8. Coming of the Holy Spirit. When the Day of Pentecost had fully come, they were all with one accord in one place. ² And suddenly there came a sound from heaven, as of a rushing mighty wind, and it filled the whole house where they were sitting. ³ Then there appeared to them divided tongues, as of fire, and *one* sat upon each of them. ⁴ And they were all filled with the Holy Spirit and began to speak with other tongues, as the Spirit gave them utterance.

The Crowd's Response ⁵And there were dwelling in Jerusalem Jews, devout men, from every nation under heaven. ⁶ And when this sound occurred, the multitude came together and they were confused because everyone heard them speak in his own language. ⁷ Then they were all amazed and marveled, saying to one another, "Look, are not all these who speak Galileans? ⁸ And how *is it that* we hear, each in our own language in which we were born?

The Scriptures are True

The scriptures are true, and as the body of Christ we need to be equipped and prepared to be empowered by the Holy Spirit so we can wield the sword when required. We need to be able to operate in full power and authority. The enemy knows scripture, has power but he does not have authority. We need to know this status to our very core and be prepared so we do not give any authority to the enemy to gain a foothold in our lives, for his agenda is specific: to steal, kill and destroy!

This is a message we need to share with everyone we know, especially in our immediate family and sphere of influence within the body of Christ.

Here's to you being filled with the Holy Spirit and blessed beyond measure so when you hear God's voice and proceed with God's wisdom you will not lean upon your own understanding (world / enemy wisdom), only upon the word of our Lord and the guidance God gives to us by and through the Holy Spirit.

Proverbs 3:5-6. Trust in the Lord with all your heart, and lean not on your own understanding. In all your ways acknowledge Him, and He shall direct your paths.

Some (sometimes all in the room) do experience the gift of laughter. God can do more in 45 seconds than most preaching of 45 minutes. This is not something to fear but something to enjoy as it is the Holy Spirit's refreshing touch exactly as the person has need. In fact, many times when I am asked to preach, the entire church goes into the gift of laughter! This is so great. God does a much better & quicker job with the people than we can as humans!

It is wonderful when God takes over. I have observed many variations on the theme, but the result is a close relationship with God and Christ through the guidance of the Holy Spirit.

Bottom line: Your life will never be the same.

I often begin the time together with the phrase: *"**It does not matter that you remember my name. What does matter is that God sent a woman your way and your life has not been the same, since that day.**"*

If you have not been around people who have invited the Holy Spirit into every fiber of their being, you may want to be sitting in a comfortable chair before you extend an invitation. Many experience what they call 'unspeakable joy' and many are filled with what is called the 'gift of laughter,' so sitting in a comfortable chair is a good option. For many, this level of joy continues to be evident in daily life for days or weeks. The glory of the LORD!

How will you know?

Well, I've met so many people who simply cannot wipe the grin off of their face. They simply cannot! They finally realize why God warned us to 'lean not on our own or man's understanding' for God wanted us to be able to access His truth, so I pray you will invite the Holy Spirit into every fiber of your being in this moment if you have not done it, yet!

Then, please bless yourself by 'resting in the presence of the Lord'. Let God's love overtake you and enjoy your special time together.

When you look back at your life, you will not want your 'old life' to be part of your future! A dear friend and pastor once described the 'noticed change' in me. When I was climbing the corporate ladder, I arrived early and stayed late. I filled my brief case every day. I often fell asleep with the contents spread out on my desk at home or across my bed, because I carried that brief case home every night, without exception, and I carried it back to the office and filled it with a new stack of 'to do' items the next day.

People thought I was brilliant (at times) while I knew I even had notes about my notes!

What the pastor stated when he introduced me, it spoke volumes to me for it resonated with me as the difference in living a la Sheila striving in the world to make some sense out of life vs. walking in faith with the guidance of the Holy Spirit: "***Watch her. You will not see her refer to a single note. When she needs to insert a fact, God pulls out the exact Rolodex card and the Holy Spirit reads it to her so she can share the exact fact with you exactly when it is needed.***"

Lord I praise you for your amazing grace, mercy and training and for not giving up on me while I was blind!

Power and Authority

God had a big job on His hands since I was raised in a conservative Lutheran synod (Scandinavian Lutheran). I thought I knew what I needed to know. I had no idea that I only knew about the Lutheran denomination and the perspective of the Lutheran denomination with the desire for ALL to be Lutheran!

My life was a typical, limited, human perspective which God had to deal with again and again (and again and again, etc.). I was attending a Scandinavian Lutheran college, Augustana (team is the

Vikings, of course), when a fellow student (I believe his name was Chuck) said he was prompted to come to my dorm and call me to the lobby each morning so he could share the glorious things God did the night before: deliverance, setting the captives free, healing the people by the laying on of hands, and proceeding with the in-filling of the Holy Spirit so all who desired to operate in the power and authority would leave the meeting blessed.

I had no idea why he sought me out. I was not linking these experiences with the days of my youth when God asked me to deliver messages to the saints. **Since I was told to stop at an early age, I stopped.**

Martin Luther *"I believe that I cannot by my own reason or strength believe in Jesus Christ, my Lord, or come to Him; but the Holy Ghost has called me by the Gospel, enlightened me with His gifts, sanctified and kept me in the true faith..."*

I did know about this quote. I did not realize my Lutheran, protestant, church training meant the denomination (one of many) lean upon man's understanding and I was leaning on man's understanding when I stopped. I did not realize that I actually leaned on my own understanding for the next couple of decades.

However, my God did not give up on me!

It took God a while to train me and help me understand that His plan and realize His plans are simple; man's are complex!

Before I embarked upon this adventurous journey with God, when I heard God say, ***"Go forth and disciple..."*** I did not have

God's perspective. I would have thought God meant for the people around the world to be discipled so they could also 'think Lutheran' and 'become Lutheran'. I have generations of hard working missionaries in my family who went out and taught the people in nations around the world while they helped some regions to become Methodist, some to become Presbyterian vs. the commission we are to proceed upon by going forth and discipling all who have ears to hear and eyes to see, to lift up those who choose Christ as their Savior and the Holy Spirit as their guide.

As a spirit filled Lutheran pastor told me, ***"You may not realize the glorious things you are sharing with me would cause nearly all Lutheran pastors to show you to the door."***

Painful to realize, but I knew he was speaking the world's truth about many of the denominations within the body of Christ, the whole church, not just the Lutheran portion of the body.

There are entire denominations who do NOT want the Holy Spirit to be mentioned. It is so sad, because without declaring Christ as our Savior and receiving the in-filling of the Holy Spirit, we lack the power and authority to deal with the schemes of the enemy!

Example: Before God arranged a trip to Africa, He sent me to meet with a different Lutheran Pastor. The pastor had just returned from the World Council of Churches. At that time, he had already served the Lutheran church for more than 45 years. He was shocked about the news of God healing the sick and doing glorious things through me because I was willing to accept God's assignments.

He said, *"You sound like Paul who represented the I am."* I told him that as believers we ALL represent our LORD, the I am. Without hesitation he said, *"No!"*

He shared details about people from India lecturing during the World Council of Churches, explaining how God is speaking to the people as the work of the mediums, channeling through a metal tube from heaven? So, I told him, *"Believers do not channel and we are not mediums nor should we listen to the mediums. The scriptures are specific."*

Then, he said, *"How can you quote scripture? Few people can lead a bible study. They need to bible scholars or have proper bible training."*

I was stunned, shocked and in tears of disbelief as he looked at his watch and quickly apologized because he had to leave for another appointment.

I went to my car and I do not know how long I sat with God and cried. During the special 'God moments when God hugs us' there are no distractions for He wraps us in His arms, in His glory. I'll share a few more of these experiences and I look forward to hearing your testimonies when God does this with and for you, also!

God shared a clear message, a poignant message. I had resisted writing anything in book form to share with the world. Why? I had so much difficulty getting publishers interested in publishing what God wants to share with the people.

In fact, I had declared to God, *"All I have is common sense. A book has to be filled with great insights, powerful and compelling content and broken down into topics before it can be distributed to people around the world."*

Well, God proved His point during the appointment with this pastor when He shared his message that afternoon as I sat in my car, *"I arranged this appointment for you. You think what I give you to share with the people in the world is common sense."*

More tears.

I have no idea how long God held me in His arms and let me cry but, the parking lot was empty when I started the car to go home.

The path was not immediately made straight after that day.

God already knew about the problem 'behind the scenes' with a publishing firm who admired my manuscripts for a few years but, they had not agreed to publish anything, yet.

God prompted me a few times to call and ask **Why.**

Finally, I did make that call.

The ministry division President told me I had to pre-sell 60,000 copies before they would agree to publish my book. The LORD told me to tell the man: *There are two problems with your plan.*

They wanted to know what the problems were but, the LORD had not revealed them to me, yet.

As I prayed and opened my mouth, the LORD revealed the first problem: **1.** *You want me to lie to 59,999 people while asking them to buy a book you will not publish until the 60,000 person agrees to buy the book.* The man merely replied, ***Wow.***

Still in prayer when the LORD told me to share the second problem: 2. *You are asking the world what you should publish instead of asking God what He wants to release to the world.*

Stunned.

If my relationship with the LORD and alignment with His plan was not important to me, I know people I could call who sell 65,000 within the week of the release of their books and I could have made a plan and arranged a different structure. However, free will keeps us aligned with the world and my desire is to be fully aligned with the LORD's will and His plan for my life for it is true: *"...ear has not heard, eye has not seen, and mind is not able to begin to conceive, the glory God has* ('in store') *prepared for those who love him."* **Lord forgive us for seeking man's approval, leaning upon and aligning with man's understanding.**

Andrew Murray *"What now is faith? Nothing other than the certainty that what God says is true."*

William J. Seymour *"The Pentecostal power, when you sum it all up, is just more of God's love. If it does not bring more love, it is simply a counterfeit."*

Chapter 5 God Provides the Catapult

There is so much we have not learned by being in the church.

As Lester Sumrall shared about his experiences during times of personal fellowship with Smith Wigglesworth and specifically at the point when he had to leave England due to the war gaining momentum in Europe, the power was evident. They went through half hour segments of Wigglesworth reading the bible, then, praying together with Wigglesworth praying a blessing over Sumrall and then, Wigglesworth read from the bible again in their first visits. During their last visit, when Sumrall confirmed he had to leave England within a few days, Wigglesworth said *"I want to pray a blessing..."* upon Sumrall while tears flowed from Wigglesworth on to the forehead and down the face of Sumrall: **"Lord let all the faith that is in my heart be in his heart. Let the** *knowledge of God that resides in me also reside in him. Let all the gifts in the spirit that function in my ministry, let them function in his life."*

Wigglesworth continued to pray over Sumrall while holding him in an embrace. Sumrall felt the holy anointing of the most high God flow into him as Wigglesworth said *"You will be blessed and faith will reside in you and you will do unusual things."*

After this prophetic word, Sumrall traveled the world.

Growing up as a pew warmer, I can confirm that shifting from a pew warmer to a spirit-filled servant of the most high God is a process. The words of blessing as Wigglesworth shared have been given to me in many nations while it had not happened in a church but, I can promise you that if you are willing to share what God does in & through you to the multitude, God will arrange the introductions & connections in the exact moment they are required.

God Introduced Me To Harald Bredesen

God knew He had a lot to do, so He decided to speed up the process by introducing me to a saved, delivered and free, spirit-filled Lutheran pastor, Harald Bredesen (1918-2006).[2]

He is dearly missed. He was an amazing man of God, a mighty disciple who fully expressed the five-fold ministry. He was unique for he was allowed to remain in his career as a Lutheran pastor after he became spirit-filled.

The diversity in the people God can introduce us to within a short time frame is amazing. God has a tremendous sense of humor!

Harald is credited with founding the Charismatic Movement globally. He served on the boards of many top international ministries, with a deep friendship for many decades with Pat Robertson at CBN, Pat Boone (credited to leading both into a relationship with the Holy Spirit), presented the Prince of Peace prize to many world leaders and to Billy Graham in 2004; served on the board of the ministry with his good friend Benny Hinn.

Every moment with Harald was filled with God's wisdom, knowledge and understanding.

During each moment I was blessed to be in the presence of the LORD and Harald (it is the best way I can describe the experience of each meeting), I could easily hear the soft whispers as Harald praised the Lord and thanked Christ with every breath.

His life was the full expression of being a spirit-filled, guided and directed man of God. Anyone who spent time with him heard him whisper, pray, praise and worship the Lord constantly while thanking Christ.

Psalms 22:3-5. But You *are* holy, enthroned in the praises of Israel. ⁴ Our fathers trusted in You; They trusted, and You delivered them. ⁵ They cried to You, and were delivered; They trusted in You, and were not ashamed.

Matthew 18:20. For where two or three are gathered together in My name, I am there in the midst of them."

Pastor Harald Bredesen
Arranges Benny Hinn TV Show Interview

The introduction to Pastor Harald Bredesen was fabulous, while the steps he took to introduce me to the people he was affiliated with became deep confirmations of what God masterfully orchestrates while we are sleeping!

A perfect example is the afternoon when Harald called to ask me if I could be ready within moments to be on the Benny Hinn TV show that evening. I was honored. However, my dress and jacket were at the dry cleaners. So, I told him I would prepare quickly and drive separately to the studio.

A dear friend picked up my dress and jacket, a jacket which is supposed to be the best TV option, aka the 'Oprah red jacket', while I prayed and prepared.

It did not occur to me that I may not have a way to enter the studio if I was arriving separate, until I was at the studio and realized the electronic entrance gate was locked.

In the same moment I pulled over to the side and prayed, God arranged for Harald Bredesen's driver to arrive. The time seemed to be less than one second. Harald smiled and motioned for me to follow his car through the gate as the gate opened. We were able to drive through the private studio gate entrance at the same time.

Harald immediately introduced me to Benny Hinn and all details were arranged. Within moments, we entered the studio and the crew directed us to the front seats. Benny Hinn introduced himself and asked a few questions. I was so excited!

God Arranged Everything for Me

Benny Hinn left the studio. He received a call from TBN.

Moments later, Benny Hinn announced there would be a change in the program because the TBN staff interviewed a man named Nasir Siddiki. They felt God wanted them to immediately send Nasir to Benny's studio to be interviewed on the program.

While we waited for Nasir to arrive, we were able to spend special time with Benny. Being with Harald and Benny at the same time was clearly a significant God moment in my life.

Then, when Nasir arrived, Benny's crew prepared the audience for the taping of the first program.

Within moments, God confirmed why I was in the audience.

I was not going to be interviewed by Benny during this taping however God needed me to be His witness.

Then, Everything Changed For Me to Become God's Witness

Nasir stated Benny shared a prophetic statement on New Year's Eve about a Muslim man coming to Christ and his name shall be called Nasir.

Benny Hinn did not remember, so he asked the studio audience if any witnesses could confirm the prophetic statement.

God prompted me to remember the specifics of the program,. I watched the program on New Year's Eve so I raised my hand. Then, I looked around and realized I was God's <u>only</u> witness within the entire studio audience that evening.

God's orchestrations are beyond our human comprehension.

God Mold Us and Form Us in Your Image

My thinking about having life figured out was all wrong. I knew I was not to lean upon our own (man's) understanding (and in this case, a woman's understanding), but I did not realize that I was leaning on it about 99% of the time!

Unaware of the truth and nothing but the truth until I realized there was nobody around who knew how to take a step. Thank God, that is when He took my hand.

There was so much I did not know. I asked God, *"**Lord, how could we be so wrong? How can we accept You, state Your word is true and yet, deny key parts of the Bible and the Holy Spirit? As a church, when did we start leaning on our own understanding instead of seeking Your truth in Your word and seeking full guidance through the Holy Spirit? When did we separate from You so much as a body of believers that some denominations refuse to believe in the Holy Spirit as Christ declared so the people lack Your power, knowledge and understanding, Your wisdom given to us through the guidance of the Holy Spirit?" Lord speak to us for we are Your people and we know many of the people are suffering and the world does not* *offer the next breath, support good health, deliverance, freedom or healing.*

May Our Life Become A Living Testimony

May our faith become so obvious to the people we see each day and may the testimony of our lives become a daily expression which we are excited to share with all who have ears to hear and eyes to see the glorious things God is doing in these days. As Paul wrote to the Ephesians, may it be the same for each of us:

<u>Prayer for Spiritual Wisdom</u>: Ephesians 1:15-23. Therefore I also, *after I heard of your faith in the Lord Jesus and your love for all the saints,* [16] *do not cease to give thanks for you, making mention of you in my prayers:* [17] *that the God of our Lord Jesus Christ, the Father of glory, may give to you the spirit of wisdom and revelation in the knowledge of Him,* [18] *the eyes of your understanding being enlightened; that you may know what is the hope of His calling, what are the riches of the glory of His inheritance in the saints,* [19] *and what is the exceeding greatness of His power toward us who believe, according to the working of His mighty power* [20] **which He worked in Christ when He raised Him from the dead and seated** *Him* **at His right hand in the heavenly** *places,* [21] *far above all principality and power and might and dominion, and every name that is named, not only in this age but also in that which is to come.* [22] *And He put all things under His feet, and gave Him to be head over all things to* *the church, ²³ which is His body, the fullness of Him who fills all in all.*

Matthew Barnett *"Faith is believing that God is going to take you places before you even get there."*

John G Lake *"I want to talk with the utmost frankness and say to you, that tongues have been the making of my ministry. It is that peculiar communication with God when God reveals to my soul the truth I utter to you day by day in the ministry. Many times, I climb out of bed, take my pencil and pad, and jot down the beautiful things of God, the wonderful things of God that He talks out in my spirit and reveals to my heart."* … *"Shortly after my entrance into the ministry of healing, while attending a service where the necessity for the Baptism of the Spirit was presented, as I knelt in prayer and re-consecration to God, an anointing of the Spirit came upon me. Waves of Holy Glory passed through my being, and I was lifted into a new realm of God's presence and power."*

Kenneth Copeland *"God's plan for your life is bigger than everything coming against it."*

Oswald Chambers *"Faith is deliberate confidence in the character of God whose ways you may not understand at the time."*

Corrie Ten Boom *"Never be afraid to trust an unknown future to a known God."*

Chapter 6 God's Assignments

**Faith Walk at Home, with a Neighbor,
or by taking the next Freeway Exit!**

You do not have to travel beyond a phone call. In fact, people have actually received my phone number and placed the call without knowing anything about me. Most of the people do not realize they are calling me to be given a word of encouragement, healed or re-directed by merely hearing God's truth for their specific issue because they were being obedient and dialing my phone number. Every conversation with family members or friends is our opportunity to change a life because travel is not required to go on a 'Faith Walk'! If you are willing God will provide the opportunity.

CAUTION: Once you say yes to the LORD, the speed at which God's orchestration unfolds will amaze you!

Example: God said, "They have 'great root beer'!"

Just before a flight to the East Coast to do something God wanted to do within His orchestration of His plan, I noticed that I started 'making it all about me'. Thankful the Holy Spirit nudged, prompted or hit me with what I refer to as a gentle hit to the head with a 2 X 4 because I was in tears while having one of my ***What have I done for you lately?*** chats with God.

It happens often, perhaps in large part due to the fact I am still learning patience. Thank God, He is patient and doesn't seem to mind that He's not done with my training program yet!

Well, within seconds, God told me to exit the freeway.

As I reached the top of the exit ramp, God prompted me to look at a fast food burger sign (In-n-Out) on the other side of the freeway. In that moment God said, *"They have great root beer."* What? God knows I love great root beer but, this was a first!

As I drove into the parking lot and headed to the drive-thru line for the great root beer, God re-directed me to park and walk in to order.

To my amazement, with the drive-thru line being very long, I was the only customer entering the building.

An employee ran to the double-door entry, opened both doors wide and welcomed me. This had not happened to me before!

Then, the same employee quickly ran back behind the line of cash registers and told me how honored he is to serve me. This was a first, also. I don't know about you, but, this level of service was a new experience for me.

I was not meaning to question God when I asked the employee if they have great root beer. The young man confirmed they do. So, I ordered the root beer.

As I completed my order, I heard a man enter and place a 'to go' order, while I was holding a cardboard cup. I had no idea how he was going to serve their 'great root beer' in a cardboard cup. As I held the cup, without moving, I heard the employee merely say, "***The soda fountain is over there, in the corner.***"

Soda fountain for 'great root beer' was my question to God while the employee merely pointed to the corner not realizing I was already having a conversation with God in my head. You see, I know God knows I do not like soda fountain drinks. But, God had a plan and He was having a different conversation with me. God wanted me to go over to the soda fountain area without delay.

As soon as I got to the corner, I heard sobbing. I looked to my right and the man who entered and placed the 'to go' order was sitting at the table next to the soda fountain. His arms were folded on the table. His face was sinking deeper & deeper while sobbing. In that moment God said, ***"You are here to pray with him."***

When the man stood up to pick up his 'to go' order, I waited to catch his eye before I spoke, "***God wants me to pray with you.***" He was trying to focus. He was red faced and the tears were still falling as he nodded. So I told him, "***I have some time if you have*** *some time."* He nodded, again, so I pointed to a table and we sat for a moment.

It was 4:30 in the afternoon.

He was hesitant to share details at first, but he finally let me know he had tried to take his life the day before (Sunday). He was unsuccessful, and, what made it worse for him was the fact he thinks that he found out nobody cares. Nobody called, emailed or sent a text to ask how he was doing.

God's quick orchestration: He was crying out to God to know somebody cares so God sent him back to the same fast-food burger location he was driving by while praying. God arranged everything at the exact same time God sent me to pray with him. God let him know He cares by telling both of us to go to the same In-n-Out burger location so he could order a 'to go' burger for his brother.

It was a time set aside by God just for this man.

It is so like God to make the entire environment disappear into a holy / glory moment for me to not realize anything around us. It's the best way I can describe the experience, as everything is white and without noises or any distractions when God is doing what God needs to do and saying what only God can say. Then, while I am still thinking the place is empty, a man hit my arm while he was trying to squeeze in next to me to sit at the next table. I had no idea why the man bumped me and made so much noise in the process until I looked up and found out the entire place was completely full of people. Not one empty seat in the place.

The result: Three 'uninterrupted hours' with God, praying with this man and listening to his heart, because it was a surprise for me to find out it was 7:30 PM!

The man wanted to ask a personal question and he said he was too embarrassed to ask me inside due to so many people in the place, so he wondered if it would be OK if he walked outside to ask me. He merely wanted to know if I will help him learn how to pray like I pray. He was embarrassed because at his advanced age (49) he was raised with only repeated, memorized prayers. He had not learned how to pray with God instead of instructing God. Now, he wanted to be able to have personal conversations with God.

Wow. Within moments God can change a life, remind me He can still send me and in the midst of each type of 'Faith Walk' God blesses the people and He re-encourages me. This time, no flight tickets were required. I merely exited a freeway per God's guidance through the Holy Spirit for some great root beer.

Ready to Begin the Walk?

Just let God know you are willing and I seriously caution you to be careful if you tell God you are willing and available within the same sentence or conversation and your bags are not packed!

As the scriptures confirm, the harvest is plentiful but the laborers are few. God will orchestrate all of the details on your behalf at warp speed once He knows you are willing to go where He needs you to go.

Example: Within moments, God orchestrated a ticket at 'will call' at the airport for me to fly to another nation. I had no idea the airport had a 'will call window'. However, as God's sense of humor and divine arrangements confirmed all I had to do was show up at the airport at oh dark thirty the next morning.

The skycaps laughed. However, they were curious so they followed me to the airline ticket desk.

Their jaws dropped when a woman at the ticket counter actually said, *"I'm the will call person for the airlines"* as she handed me a ticket.

Have to admit, that statement stopped me in my tracks. I was not able to give my luggage to the skycap so I was lugging some significant luggage since the temperature change on the other side of the globe required heavy suits and coats.

Clearly, I was stunned.

My suitcases dropped to the floor.

The woman could tell. She merely smiled and asked if I was Sheila Holm.

Still stunned, I nodded 'mechanically' as she handed me the ticket. Then, just as fast as she appeared, she was gone.

Another employee walked out and asked for my ticket so she could place the tags on my suitcases and arrange my boarding pass.

It was obvious the two skycaps were still 'in awe' while they lifted and placed my bags on the scale without saying a word.

The woman who issued the ticket was not at the counter after the ticket was issued.

God's orchestrations surpass human understanding / comprehension. We serve an awesome God!

Lord be with me, always, send me where you need me to be in the world, protected by the blood of my Savior, Jesus Christ, while I remain aligned with your will, so your purpose and plan for my life will be fulfilled. Amen.

Rick Renner "*Faith is the spark that ignites the impossible and causes it to become possible. When a person's faith is activated, it sets in motion supernatural power that enables that person to do what he normally would never be able to do!*"

Corrie Ten Boom "*Is prayer your steering wheel or your spare tire?*"

Oswald Chambers "*We lean to our own understanding, or we bank on service and do away with prayer, and consequently by succeeding in the external we fail in the eternal, because in the eternal we succeed only by prevailing prayer.*"

Frederick Franson "*If you are sick, fast and pray; if the language is hard to learn, fast and pray; if the people will not hear you, fast and pray, if you have nothing to eat, fast and pray*"

Chapter 7 Activation of Faith

It is important to remove the thoughts which would cause you to think some Christians operate at different levels. As I describe God's masterful orchestration, it is critical to realize I am human and God works through me in ways that cause me to stand in awe and yet, at any moment in time I can be so human. It can be a fine line. Sometimes people become what is known as 'so heavenly minded they are no earthly good' because they quote scripture or what God told them when they needed an answer and they cannot relate to human issues in the moment. Grateful God keeps it real!

I remember a time when I was in tears. I had no 'good food' in the house. I munched on some carrots which were in the refrigerator way too long. They made me so sick. As soon as I was able to place a call, I called a man God introduced me to, a man who had been a blessing to me and to my ministry for a long time. I trusted he would have an encouraging word.

However, what I heard was not a message which seemed encouraging in the moment.

He actually told me he experienced this type of situation in his life. They had young daughters at the time and both were in diapers. There were no more diapers or food in the house, so his wife put on her best dress, laid down on the bed and told him she was ready for Jesus to come.

As soon she told him, he heard their doorbell. He went to the door and a woman handed him grocery bags and asked if he would help unload the rest of the bags from her car. The woman provided more than food for the family because God prompted her to buy the exact needs for the family including the two sizes and brands of diapers they had used for their daughters.

He said the Lord would do the same for me. I prayed!!!

Within a moment, I heard my doorbell. A woman stopped by to pick me up because some women were going together to hear Rodney Howard-Browne and they wanted me to join them.

God prompted me to grab some of the scarves I sell when I speak.

That night women purchased the scarves. I received exactly the amount needed to purchase what I would need for the next journey, to rent a car to take me to the airport and enough to purchase something to eat and provide a blessing as an abundant tip when we stopped to eat and fellowship together. God provided more than enough!

The Faith Walk is 'Activation of Faith, One Step at a Time'!

Man's plan had destroyed every aspect of my life. I knew in God I had hope and a future and yet, I was not aware of what was possible if I would grasp God's hand and go on a 'Faith Walk!'

Arrangements

God arranged for a training structure which became a global 'Faith Walk'.

God made all of the arrangements: flight tickets, introductions to the people in each of the nations before my arrival, accommodations everywhere He arranged for me to go and all of the various transportation needs, plus all communication and financial arrangements without my help or assistance while preparing me to be launched forth through my 'bouts of resistance'.

Each time God made the arrangements for the assignment, I did not immediately jump up and down and say, *"**Yes Lord, send me.**"*

It took a while for me to shift from concern to being in awe.

Yes. I resisted. Why? I am human. I did not realize I actually resisted God's plan each time but, I know I was feeling unqualified to proceed. Training to know that I know He will never leave or forsake me was was not easy for our LORD to accomplish at first.

Regardless, God persevered through it all. God was willing to train me 'on the go', and His plan meant I was in for an amazing series of journeys! And, He will do the same with and for you!

A little recap which confirms the truth for believers. We are to walk in the spirit and not in the flesh (world), for we are in the world but, we are not of the world.

Romans 8: *There is* therefore now no condemnation to those who are in Christ Jesus, who do not walk according to the flesh, but according to the Spirit. ^{2} For the law of the Spirit of life in Christ Jesus has made me free from the law of sin and death. ^{3} For what the law could not do in that it was weak through the flesh, God *did* by sending His own Son in the likeness of sinful flesh, on account of sin: He condemned sin in the flesh, ^{4} that the righteous requirement of the law might be fulfilled in us who do not walk according to the flesh but according to the Spirit.

^{5} For those who live according to the flesh set their minds on the things of the flesh, but those *who live* according to the Spirit, the things of the Spirit. ^{6} For to be carnally minded *is* death, but to be spiritually minded *is* life and peace. ^{7} Because the carnal mind *is* enmity against God; for it is not subject to the law of God, nor indeed can be.

^{8} So then, those who are in the flesh cannot please God. ^{9} But you are not in the flesh but in the Spirit, if indeed the Spirit of God dwells in you. Now if anyone does not have the Spirit of Christ, he is not His.

^{10} And if Christ *is* in you, the body *is* dead because of sin, but the Spirit *is* life because of righteousness.

^{11} But if the Spirit of Him who raised Jesus from the dead dwells in you, He who raised Christ from the dead will also give life to your mortal bodies through His Spirit who dwells in you. ^{12} Therefore, brethren, we are debtors—not to the flesh, to live according to the flesh. ^{13} For if you live according to the flesh you will die; but if by the Spirit you put to death the deeds of the body, you will live. ¹⁴ For as many as are led by the Spirit of God, these are sons of God. ¹⁵ For you did not receive the spirit of bondage again to fear, but you received the Spirit of adoption by whom we cry out, "Abba, Father."

¹⁶ The Spirit Himself bears witness with our spirit that we are children of God, ¹⁷ and if children, then heirs—heirs of God and joint heirs with Christ, if indeed we suffer with *Him,* that we may also be glorified together. ¹⁸ For I consider that the sufferings of this present time are not worthy *to be compared* with the glory which shall be revealed in us.

¹⁹ For the earnest expectation of the creation eagerly waits for the revealing of the sons of God. ²⁰ For the creation was subjected to futility, not willingly, but because of Him who subjected *it* in hope; ²¹ because the creation itself also will be delivered from the bondage of corruption into the glorious liberty of the children of God. ²² For we know that the whole creation groans and labors with birth pangs together until now.

²³ Not only *that,* but we also who have the first fruits of the Spirit, even we ourselves groan within ourselves, eagerly waiting for the adoption, the redemption of our body. ²⁴ For we were saved in this hope, but hope that is seen is not hope; for why does one still hope for what he sees? ²⁵ But if we hope for what we do not see, we eagerly wait for *it* with perseverance.

²⁶ Likewise the Spirit also helps in our weaknesses. For we do not know what we should pray for as we ought, but the Spirit Himself makes intercession for us with groanings which cannot be uttered.

²⁷ Now He who searches the hearts knows what the mind of the Spirit *is,* because He makes intercession for the saints according to *the will of* God. ²⁸ And we know that all things work together for good to those who love God, to those who are the called according to *His* purpose.

²⁹ For whom He foreknew, He also predestined *to be* conformed to the image of His Son, that He might be the firstborn

among many brethren. ³⁰ Moreover whom He predestined, these He also called; whom He called, these He also justified; and whom He justified, these He also glorified.

Flight Tickets & Hotels & Transportation

When the employees with the airlines knew God needed me to be half way around the world in three days, they were shocked I would simply ask the airlines for a ticket but, after the ninth employee stated, *"It would take a miracle..."* my request resulted in God's plan and provision being confirmed: <u>I was given a ticket by the Supervisor / Manager and the staff met me at the airport</u>!

FYI: I tried a little bit of a Sheila plan by saying, *I'll sit in the jump seat.* God had to be laughing because I was immediately informed I would have to know how to fly the plane if something happened to the pilot during the flight. Yikes!

This was not due to the efforts of the prior nine employees. Each employee who said, *"It will take a miracle to get you there..."* caused me to build my faith with each response when God confirmed, *"Great, because I live based on miracles."* The woman who granted the ticket wanted to hear more details about God needing me to be in Australia within three days.

Hotel Room & Transportation

Since I would arrive in Sydney the night before the Pastor, a hotel room was reserved for me by his ministry team. However, I was informed that I would need to pay the fee which was estimated at one hundred dollars. I had no option to cover the bill, so even though the flight was arranged I told God I would not be able to go. Again, however, God confirmed it was already arranged.

God told me to go to the Post Office box before the flight early on Sunday morning.

It was already late Saturday night when I was informed about the hotel bill. Without a moment's hesitation, I did it. I leaned on my own understanding. For you see, I quickly leaned on my own understanding because I knew how the mail system worked. I had checked my mail on Friday. The 'business mail' is Monday through Friday. Therefore, in my mind, I knew there was no option for resolving a financial need at the Post Office.

However, since God knew the full plan and I dismissed the 'something in the mail' option, God merely prompted me again to get to the Post Office.

To my complete surprise, a check issued by a major American bank which is recognized globally was waiting for me at the Post Office. It was a dividend check from a client who was not able to pay a fee when I helped establish his business so he agreed to pay stock dividends in the future. This was the first dividend check.

The check was all I had 'in hand' when I flew to Australia in awe of how God was going to work it all out since I did not have a bank or credit account and I did not know if the hotel would cash the check before I arrived. Again, I was back to leaning upon my own understanding in the same moment I was boarding the plane in faith. We are such funny people when we are operating as limited humans!

When we landed in Australia, I asked a shuttle driver how far I would need to walk to get to the hotel.

The man said he could provide transportation. I hesitated.

Since the check was for only a little over the one hundred dollars required for the hotel room, I explained what was going on and that I would not want him to take me if I could not pay him for the trip.

The man was immediately enrolled in the process. He wanted to know what God was doing. It was the end of his shift and he would take me to the hotel whether he was going to be paid or not.

Since the check was from a bank recognized globally, the hotel cashed the check. And, to my complete surprise, God provided the exact amount required in 'Australian dollars' to meet the need: 1. Hotel bill, paid, 2. Shuttle to the hotel, paid; 3. Snack (apple) at the hotel, paid; 4. Shuttle back to the airport to meet the pastor in the morning, paid (the shuttle driver was going to be 'off shift' but he volunteered to pick me up as he wanted to meet the pastor and hear more details about what God was orchestrating); 5. Breakfast prior to going to the airport, paid; the exchange rate of American dollars to Australian dollars provided exactly the amount needed to proceed upon the journey.

When I laughed with God about this, it was clear I was always thinking American. God showed me in this instance and in many other examples that a 'Faith Walk' is based upon God's currency and not ours!

Introductions

God introduced me to people in nations before I arrived.

He introduced me to nations I had not heard of before God arranged the assignment.

One time I was caught by surprise. Everyone was saying, *"Sheila."* I was shocked. I could have become prideful as everyone was saying it even though my resume was just sent by fax a day or two prior to my arrival. Then, the truth in several nations provided a personal humbling moment: *"Any gal is a Sheila."*

That's right, the next time you go to an Outback Steakhouse look at the bathroom door for all of the gals: *Sheilas.*

Bishop George Dallas McKinney
Prays Over Introductory Letter and Reveals Specifics
God Arranges for Me to Become God's Witness
And, the Witness for Bishop McKinney at the Same Time!

Often, I heard the name Bishop McKinney as I traveled the world. I did not know Bishop McKinney before God arranged global travel. As soon as I returned to San Diego, a man called to confirm we could meet while he was going to be in San Diego to attend a board meeting with Bishop McKinney. Wow. Finally, a chance to meet the man I heard about so often as I traveled.

It was a stormy day with heavy rain. I did not care. I circled the building a few times before I was directed by a man to take the parking space directly in front of the building. I apologized to the man at the door, since I felt the space would be needed for someone attending the special board meeting but, I confirmed I would only be there for a minute or two to hopefully meet Bishop McKinney.

By this time, I was busy helping churches in trouble and re-encouraging pastors in the area, and even though I knew a spirit-filled Lutheran pastor, he merely confirmed what I already knew: ***"Most Lutheran pastors hearing about the glorious details you are sharing with me would show you the door,"*** while I prayed God would direct me to a church that would understand me, a place where I could be blessed and soak in truth so I would have a church home.

The man who directed me to the parking place merely took my hand in his and said, ***"For the Lord would have you know I am Bishop McKinney, I understand you and you have a church home here."*** The man who came out in the rain to help me ... I was talking with Bishop McKinney!

I could not talk in logical phrases let alone construct a sentence while he handed me a few pamphlets he authored. I noticed the address on the material and for the first time I realized Bishop McKinney is a pastor in San Diego. He told me to call his assistant and tell her that I am to meet with him in three days. I merely nodded and left.

For the next three days, I typed. I did not take many breaks to have a snack, and I did not sleep. I typed.

Each time I asked God what He wanted me to share with Bishop McKinney, God confirmed another location in the world where God had arranged for me to travel, to pray with the people, to re-encourage pastors, to meet with their boards and deacons to share the message God had for them, and to help God's people, church to church, business to business and nation to nation.

The introductory letter for Bishop McKinney was the initial manuscript for this book. I only had time to take a quick shower and dab a bit of make-up on my face while the manuscript pages were being printed from my computer before it was time for me to put a few hair clips in my hair in an attempt to style my wet hair because it was time to drive to Bishop McKinney's office.

As I entered Bishop's office, he accepted the stack of pages, turned them upside down on his desk, laid his hands upon them and prayed. From the first page to the last, Bishop identified every person and ministry. I did not identify the men's ministry, but Bishop did as I immediately said, *"It's in there, but I did not identify the ministry by name."*

Bishop smiled as he said, *"Thank you. I'm the Chaplain for Promise Keepers. The message was needed. The ministry was in trouble at that time. Thank you."*

Bishop went through the entire manuscript without reading a word of it, and he specifically identified the details in the exact order which they appeared in the manuscript. He knew the ministries by name, and he stated the names of the people as though he was reading the details on the pages.

In fact, he thanked me for being the witness to the King's coronation in Africa as I repeated my surprised response, *"It's in there, but I did not identify the person or ministry by name."* The man, Kingsley Fletcher, was Bishop's friend of more than 15 years and Bishop was not able to go to the coronation so he prayed God would send a witness. Bishop was thanking me as that witness.

In each of these moments, I stood in awe of the depth of wisdom from the LORD shared with Bishop. We serve an awesome God!

Prayer Friend and Pilot in Texas Arranges Tour of TBN
Introductions Arranged by God

During a brief layover in Dallas, between flights, I was asked to pray for a man, a pilot, John Willison. He's a man with a mighty testimony.[3] God had a deep message for me to share with John.

We met through friends who picked me up at the Dallas airport and drove me to a restaurant to pray with their friend, John.

Within moments, God confirmed we needed to pray in a more private setting so we went to John's home.

The prayer specifics were overheard and identified by John's house guest as the exact vision God had given to John, a vision John had set aside.

This introduction to John turned into multiple introductions by John and his house guest, an amazing singer, Earl Harrigan, during an extended time in Dallas and points beyond with John as our pilot.

John felt it would be good to arrange for a tour of TBN in Irving, Texas, on our way to the Day Star TV show taping with singer Earl Harrigan.

As soon as we entered the side door of TBN, Phil and Hazel, the brother and sister-in-law of Paul Crouch, met us and thanked us for coming. Before I was introduced, they said God sent me to pray with one of their staff members. They were going to clear the prayer room, but God confirmed the office of the person should be the location so I said it was not necessary to clear the prayer room. I asked if the person has an office and they confirmed the details while directing me to the specific location. Prayers continued for a woman while she proceeded to kick the lower right desk drawer open until she went through two boxes of Kleenex.

Due to the hours at TBN, we missed the opportunity to be at Day Star TV taping as planned. However, God introduced me to the producer of TBN's **Praise the Lord** by arranging for the invitation to pray with her in her office. She scheduled me for future interview tapings of **Praise the Lord** in Irving, TX. I was thrilled. However, it was a bit of a distance to travel and arrange for hotel stays due to not being taped in the studio within a few miles from my home in California. God orchestrated the flights, introductions, sharing with new friends and family in Christ plus the hotel stays as required, with precision. The first taping resulted in an invitation to be with a special singer featured on TBN, Jana Jay (now Jana Offutt), to meet her family and enjoy their weekend performance in **The Promise.** While I was with Jana, the National

Coordinator for Kenneth Copeland Ministries called. She saw me on TBN and the ministry invited me to share the platform with Jesse DuPlantis on Sunday morning. The service was part of the annual Kenneth Copeland gathering of partners so it was an amazing and blessed experience.

The second TBN taping matched the schedule for the Benny Hinn partner weekend so I was invited to sit with the ministry staff. God's orchestrations are beyond human comprehension and I am truly the fortunate one! The location of Pastor Benny's meeting was the church located on the TBN studio lot. God arranged for the exact amount required for a hotel stay so I could remain to enjoy the additional meetings within the special ministry section a second night. Amazing blessings!

Henrietta Mears *"Faith is caught rather than taught."*

Proverbs 3:5-6. Trust in the Lord with all your heart, And lean not on your own understanding; In all your ways acknowledge Him, And He shall direct your paths.

Martin Luther *"I believe that I cannot by my own reason or strength believe in Jesus Christ, my Lord, or come to Him; but the Holy Ghost has called me by the Gospel, enlightened me with His gifts, sanctified and kept me in the true faith..."*

Joni Eareckson Tada *"Faith isn't the ability to believe long and far into the misty future. It's simply taking God at His Word and taking the next step."*

Chapter 8   God's Plans are Big

We may not remember the plans God has for us.

May God remind you of the plans He has for you!

Jeremiah 29:11-13. *For I know the thoughts that I think toward you, says the Lord, thoughts of peace and not of evil, to give you a future and a hope. [12] Then you will call upon Me and go and pray to Me, and I will listen to you. [13] And you will seek Me and find Me, when you search for Me with all your heart.*

God Had To Remind Me:
Faith Walk Request Started When I Was Four

God arranged for me to see a vision of the past (it was just like watching a movie of our farm and how it all looked when I was a young child) so I would remember what I said I would do.

God reminded me of an encounter when I was four. We lived on a farm. I was marching in our meadow with my curly, wavy auburn red hair blowing in the wind and I was repeating and repeating one statement with great intensity: *"**They're really nice people but they just don't get it.**"*

Then, in a second, I was flat on my back in the tall grass when God asked, *"**Don't you want to do what I want you to do?**"*

I remembered having a large smile on my face as I say, *"**I will do anything you want me to do!**"*

How do I remember it so well? Each time God hears me doing some version of my 'resistance song and dance' regarding His request for me to take on a new assignment, God shows me responding to His request from His perspective. Tears are flowing down each side of my face as I am in the special glorious moments with Him, saying, *"**I'll do anything you want me to do.**"*

It was not easy for me to say yes at first, especially since I knew 'more qualified' candidates to send! It was not clear to me that God needed me to go on the assignment. In fact, I actually spent time 'splainin' to God' that nobody will believe this actually happened to me when I was four.

So, what did God do? God immediately arranged for me to meet four year olds in various countries while God arranged travel nation to nation. God spoke to the four year olds who prepared 'in advance of my arrival' to confirm they hear from God. Each one was told about my experience with God when I was four!

When I asked God how I was supposed to remember what I was doing and thinking and saying when I was four, God introduced me to many four year olds.

Now, God has revealed, *"**You were predestined to fulfill upon your plan and purpose.**"* God showed me many examples where I made a choice to be worldly successful vs remain aligned with His plan. Trusted I upset God too much. However, He reminded me, *"**I've always been this close to you. I've never left you and I will never forsake you.**"*

Initially, I was challenged by so many people I became a bit confused so I asked God again, *"**How would I remember things when I am four ... I was a child ... scripture says when we are children, we speak and act like children ...**"*

God was clear in His response, *"**The children are to come unto me. To Me, you are My child every day of your life.**"*

Wow. I was told God did not need me by so many people I thought were knowledgeable, I put distance between myself and God.

More prayers were required because evidently, with this realization boldly brought to my attention, I needed to become more bold about God's truth when I am in conversation with people and I had some restructuring to do in my life!

God is so good, He gently and slowly shows us the truth when we are willing. I thought I was always willing to hear God's plans.

I am so grateful God knows exactly how to redirect us aka snap us back to reality when it is required!

God arranged for each four year old to draw the exact same picture of the farm as it appeared when I was four, positioning a house, a barn, a cow, a horse, rows of trees (the wind break around the main buildings during the severe winters) and a girl in the meadow with the bright light shining upon me from heaven. I received this picture from: 1. a boy in Australia, 2. a girl, the daughter of the associate pastor of a church in East London, and then, 3. A Dutch Reformed girl who instructed her Mom to go to the exact church in California where I was going to be on the exact Sunday when I was visiting the church.

During the third experience, I was thanking God for the children and asking God to confirm the children at that age know how to hear His voice, praise Him and speak to Him as their Father. While I was still in my conversation with God He sent another four year old girl to me, to present me with a gift. The girl handed me her 'old' tambourine. I was surprised. The girl was very serious that God wanted me to have her 'old' tambourine.

Within moments, her mother joined us and explained the details. Christina Thee (Christ in thee) had just turned four. They were amazed when they asked her what she wanted for her 4th birthday, because she only said, *"A new tambourine. I want a new one to praise God with."*

So, they bought her a new tambourine and some other items they knew she would enjoy, and they asked her, *"What do you want us to do with the old one?"* Christina said, *"I need to leave it at church. God is sending someone to the church ..."* They had waited patiently to see what she would do with her tambourine, and they were amazed when she walked up to me because she was determined and quick with her delivery and that is not like her as she did not know me.

By the way, she was wearing 'Wizard of Oz Dorothy red sequin slippers' which was one of the special gifts she received for her birthday. When I told her they were absolutely beautiful, God prompted me to ask her why she enjoyed them so much. She said, *"It reminds me of home ...* (and then, she leaned in close and whispered) ... *we are never too far away from home ... God is right here, all the time ... sometimes, we just forget."*

The wisdom. It rendered me speechless.

Christina is a precious soul. Her mother shared an experience on the playground at the daycare the previous week. A little girl fell and cut herself. When Christina noticed the blood she prayed, *"God heal her in Jesus' name."* The daycare suspended Christina for praying on the playground. ***Lord, help us!*** I spent some time praying with Christina, hearing her heart and offering 'for now' to pray privately to God for He will honor her prayers. I asked her to pray that more adults will stand up for the rights of Christians to be able to pray openly without restrictions. ***Lord, hear our prayers!***

In another church, God directed my attention to a girl in front of me with long, curly and wavy auburn red hair who knelt to pray during the service. The rest of the congregation was oblivious to the intense prayers of this young girl. When she stood up she told her mom, **"The pastor's dad is going to be OK."** The little girl wanted her parents to deliver the message to the pastor. Her parents were hesitant about giving the message to the pastor so they told her they were sure the pastor knows because God would tell him, also. The little girl said, **"God has been telling him but he does not believe it. He is doubting God."**

God gave me the opportunity to speak with her parents and to encourage them, as I did with each of the parents who have children sensitive to God's voice. Each time, I confirmed it will help if you ask your children each morning what God has been sharing with them. They will be honest and direct about God's messages. Each time, I was able to share the testimony of when I was young and I had messages. I was told, **"If God has a message for them, God will tell them."** I was the obstinate red head who responded, **"They need to know God is speaking to them, he's shouting in their ears but they are not listening."**

Another Unique Example:
God Speaking Directly to the Children

While speaking in a church in California, I trusted God had fired me! My host family, dear friends and parents of a four year old daughter arranged for me to speak on a Saturday evening at their local church.

Their daughter was already a special prayer warrior at her young age (a.k.a., in her 4th year; I met her when she was only a few months old), Collynn Young, daughter of Pastor Greg and Patricia Young.

She desperately wanted to hear me speak but, due to her age, the youth care-takers sent her to a play room.

Well, I did not know the timing of the evening. So, I trusted I was done after I spoke for 45 minutes. Plus, the pastor was leaving. However, the pastor stated he had another meeting to attend and the people confirmed they did not want me to stop. So, I prayed as nobody was taking an offering and there is clearly a scripture about the worker being worth their hire. I asked the Lord, *If the costs for me to be here were not going to be handled by an offering then, have you fired me?*

The people wanted more, so I continued for another 45 minutes. Then, they still did not want to take a break. They wanted to continue, so we continued. Then, a man asked to be excused briefly to pick up his daughter, since it was almost 10 PM and the mall was closing at 10 PM. So, when I realized the time, again, I trusted we should stop. But, the group did not want to stop, so we continued. We joined together in a prayer circle after the man returned from the mall and his teenage daughter wanted to participate. We concluded the meeting in prayer at about 10:30.

Throughout the evening, I kept asking God, *"Am I fired? A worker is worth their hire – it says it in scripture. They want more and more and they did not take an offering, so tell me loudly, so I hear you ... am I fired?"* I listened intently until I drifted off to sleep. God was silent.

The next morning, I thought I heard some light footsteps in the hallway. I was on the living room sofa, while I was being hosted. I started to open my eyes. when I heard soft whispers, *"Oh, good. You are awake. Good. I need to tell you something and I've waited all night."* Collynn was so determined, I had to smile.

"Let me sit up a bit, first, OK?" I said, while she said, *"OK, but, hurry up, please."*

She was so excited she quickly leaned over the sofa bed to whisper in my ear, while almost falling on top of me, *"God wants you to know you are not fired."*

Shocked to hear it so clearly from her, while I actually said, *"Really?"*

"Yes. So, can I ask you something?" as she leaned back a bit, to look me eye to eye. I nodded yes, so she asked, *"What does fired mean?"*

Oh, our Lord does speak to four year olds and he does have a fabulous sense of humor!

I asked her to tell me why she waited all night. She told me she tried to leave the play room, because she wanted to hear me speak, but she was told she is too young so she would not be able to leave the play room to be with adults.

Then, when God told her, ***"Tell Sheila she is not fired,"*** she told the woman in charge that she had to go to the meeting because God wanted her to deliver a message to Sheila. But, the woman would not let her leave the play room. Since Collynn was not supposed to disturb the meeting of the adults and she insisted she had to deliver the message, they made her Mother take her home and she went to bed before I returned to the house. So, she apologized that she had to go home and not tell me, because then, she had to wait all night to tell me what God wanted her to tell me!

Thank God for the children! And, may we learn a lesson from this experience. May we ask the Holy Spirit what is going on and allow the Holy Spirit to speak to us vs. leaning upon our own understanding!

Come to Christ as Children for
God's Plans are Bigger and Better!

God took me global to get me away from the day to day of my debacle but, a Faith Walk with God is something that He hungers to do with each of us and it does not require global travel. To prepare to launch means you are willing to let God grasp your hand and take you on the journey of your life. The choice is yours. I pray you will say, ***"YES."***

Then, send me your story, your testimony, because God has arranged for a series of books to be released which will provide our testimonies as we take a 'Faith Walk' as a parent, a pastor, a teen, a teacher, etc.

Praying with you as you embark upon the path God has prepared for you!

Matthew Barnett *"Faith is believing that God is going to take you places before you even get there."*

2 Corinthians 5:7. For we walk by faith, not by sight.

Habakkuk 2:3 Faith in God includes Faith in His timing.

Smith Wigglesworth *"There are two kinds of faith. There is the natural faith. But the supernatural faith is the gift of God."*

"We become supernatural by the power of God. We find this power working through every part of our being "

Chapter 9 Jonah and the Whale

I pray you will take God's hand and go for a 'Faith Walk' without so much resistance! At first, it did not seem like I was resisting God. Sometimes, I felt I was merely 'advising God', doing all I could to be steadfast and diligent in the process, while not realizing I was actually questioning God's authority and decision making if He did not send one of the candidates I mentioned, people I felt were far more qualified.

At first, I thought I had a great excuse. Remember, I was raised as a Scandinavian Lutheran! I reminded God on a frequent basis. Thank God, God is patient and He has a great sense of humor.

If I had a penny for each time I reminded God of the facts I knew, the many reasons why I was not qualified … even though business coaching clients refer to me the Professor of Profitability, because I am someone who can stretch a penny so much it turns into copper wire and becomes far more valuable.

Sad, but, God had to spend time reminding me about all of the input He imparted to me since the date He sent me to my family. And, the farm training was exactly what blesses me when God places me in unique nations which are not modernized. God put a lot of effort into making me adaptable so I could represent Him wherever He sends me to be on the soil where he places my feet.

God used a constant example of 'Jonah and the whale'. And, when I say constant in God's terms I trust you are beginning to realize it was like seeing a billboard message without a billboard!

It finally became comical and then, it became the depth of the initial journey.

God delivered his 'Jonah and the whale' messages through new sources in new ways each and every time until I was 'on assignment'.

That's right. More than three years of hearing the same words after every prophetic word or vision shared: ***"God wants me to remind you about the three days Jonah spent in the whale. He said you would understand."***

Even when I accepted the assignment, God had more to share with me about 'Jonah and the whale'.

Just when I thought I knew the story, God showed me more and more depth within the message. Jonah continued to be the theme even after I completed the assignment, because God had more to reveal to me about the full story of Jonah. Only four chapters but, it is a powerful book in the bible!

For now, it is important to realize that it took a while for me to pull away from what people said to me and about me in the world and fully grasp the concept that God felt I was ready. I had spent so much time chatting with God about what I needed to do to get ready, without realizing I was trying to inform God of his requirements to fulfill upon before God could launch me.

The joke was on me. I had no idea what God was doing to train me. I had so much to learn. But, what was I thinking? Looking back, it does seem silly but, I did not realize how ridiculous it was at the time.

My input, aka my interference, actually delayed the launch date from three days to three years. Who was I listening to? Man, also known as the enemy speaking through others to counter what the LORD was revealing to me while most of the people were truly well meaning Christians who were very interested in advising me of God's requirements:

1. You will need at least eight to thirteen years of mentoring by a man of authority within the body of Christ before God can launch you.

God merely responded, *"Is man sending you forth or am I?"*

2. You are not to go out alone, as a lone ranger. You will appear to be a loose cannon and have no credibility within the body of Christ.

God merely responded, *"Did I send two tickets to Australia, London, Africa, or did I send one?"*

3. You do not have any published books when you speak, so you are not considered an authority on any subject within the body of Christ, yet.

God merely responded, *"We do not need to sell books to go where I need you to go ... to do what I need you to do."*

4. You would not be launched to a men's ministry to advise them because God would send a man.

Again, silly me, but, I became busy researching and referring top men in the body of Christ to God on a regular basis, especially highlighting the many accomplishments of well known authors and speakers, the specific men I felt would be well qualified and they were clearly ready for God to send to send them. But, when I referred them to God, God confirmed he asked each one and they said, *"No."* Shocked; I told God I had no idea how they could all tell Him *"No."*

God immediately corrected my thinking by reminding me how each time I am resisting His assignment, I am telling God *"No."*

Ouch! God stunned me with this one!

It was not that 'easy' for God to launch me forth.

My immediate (and I felt 100% valid) question was due to not feeling qualified for God to launch me to a men's ministry. Even though God was validating me, I leaned on man's understanding.

God's response to my concern: God wanted me to represent Him. It was not about me! Plus, He was doing more to train me and prepare me to go, way beyond a little bit of gentle nudging.

Justification for this assignment was tough in my mind, even though I spoke at conferences, because I knew a lot of great men in the leadership of the body of Christ, and clearly they were more qualified, especially to be sent to a Men's ministry.

So, without realizing my approach, I reverted to Sheila logic, and I began submitting references to God, in the hopes (and with a clear understanding inside my mind that I was right) God would send one of the qualified men I brought to his attention. It took the entire three years of this process, before I finally realized I was referring powerful men of God that God already knew and realized He could send.

The entire three years, God kept sending people to me to tell me about the story of Jonah in the whale. After God sent a few people to share parts of the story, God started sending people to merely remind me about the three days of Jonah in the whale which was a confirmation of His message being shared through the person.

Then, while I was speaking at a conference, God sent the same message through three people from various states to confirm God wanted me to attend a women's conference. I'm a single woman and I do not have children so I trusted I did not have any personal information to share, for me to be a contribution or blessing, and I trusted God would agree.

I was wrong.

God did not agree with me, at all.

Before I realized it, I started bargaining with God to send me to any business conference, any business meeting, to speak on any topic about business and I would be ready to go without hesitation. It was a safe place for me and I personally trusted God would eventually agree. Hoping very soon God would be smiling.

However, I was wrong.

Evidently, I was oblivious, again, not realizing that I was questioning God's wisdom, again.

While I continued to ask God, *"What would they benefit from me attending?"* God confirmed my availability to go.

Then, my cousin and prophetic prayer partner, Rozanne, called.

Her closest prayer partner had registered me for the conference.

God had arranged for her to take care of all registration details until she hit a road block. God directed her attention to the conference web site while He only confirmed: ***Register your prayer partner's cousin for the women's conference in Southern California.*** The woman did not know my name to complete the registration so she provided my cousin's name and phone number.

We serve an awesome God!

Important to remember: ***We do not know what the LORD is orchestrating 'in advance' of walking forward in faith.***

God has a sense of humor. I only knew the training phase from the blessing side and I really enjoyed the fact He would fill me and restore me every time I proceeded to bless as He directed.

Now, the training program was changing. The conference had nothing to do with what I could share or what I could do to bless. The LORD was divinely orchestrating a blessing for me if I would merely agree show up!

My cousin knew something amazing was going to happen due to the LORD providing a way through her prayer partner so she was very excited. The conference was within a couple of days so I was out of time to resist or think about options because the LORD knew I was clearly available.

Fabulous women attended. Some of us prayed together, and some of us ministered to each other. I was deeply blessed. God knew before I arrived that I always seek ways to bless, but now, the roles were reversed? Shocked! As the hours passed, it was clear that I was blessed 'beyond measure'. In fact, per my 'can I take in more blessings' meter, I was ready to explode!

On the last full day of the conference, I told God that I would stay for the afternoon session, and then I would go home immediately after. I was not part of the organization so I did not see a reason to return in the morning for the final session.

However, as soon as the session began, a woman ran up to the front of the room. She grabbed the microphone, nearly shouting her first words which were clearly words for me (may not be 100%

of what she shared however since it was not taped and I was in a bit of shock when I realized it was a personal word for me): *"I've not shared a word from the Lord for twelve years because the last word I shared was not accepted when a person stated to the pastor he did not think the word I was sharing was from the Lord.*

I would not be up here right now, however, this is a word for someone here, someone God wants to bless and you are not planning to stay after the session, so God wants me to share this word of truth and knowledge with you right now for He confirmed the person would understand:

God showed me a vision of a courtroom.

God told me that He wants you to know He was with you when you experienced a tragic judgment in the courtroom.

God told me it was so severe, He wants you to know that even He cried.

God wants you to picture that courtroom now. As you walk into the courtroom, God wants you to line up all of the defendants in front of you. Then, starting from the left, God wants you to look deeply into the eyes of the first person until you can forgive them. Then, look as deeply into the next persons' eyes, and the next, each time long enough until you forgive them.

You do not realize that you are so busy looking into the eyes of each man that you do not notice Jesus has walked into the courtroom.

In fact, Jesus is whispering in your ear, standing next to you, before you realize He is with you while He asks you, "Perhaps you are sitting in my seat?"

You didn't even realize you had positioned yourself in the judges' seat, but, now that you do, you quickly move out of the seat and let Jesus sit in the judges' seat.

Then, as you look at the defendants, you are ready to hear the judgment of Jesus Christ, so you begin to feel so proud of yourself that Jesus will sit in judgment that you are not focused upon Jesus the first time He asks the question of you, until you hear Jesus repeat His one question, "Will you let me forgive them, as deeply as I have forgiven you?"

In this moment, I could not stop the tears…I could not move.

God worked diligently to send me to this conference, so this woman could be re-encouraged after 12 years, to be restored and strengthened to once again share a word of truth and knowledge from the Lord to me because I would clearly understand as I had lived the experience. Through this word, God shared His wisdom and blessed me, deeply!

As the woman left the podium, I looked at her until our eyes connected and I mouthed the words **"Thank you. Bless you."** to thank her for sharing God's word. This also let her know I would like to talk with her after the session.

God wanted her to know how deeply she had touched my life by personally delivering God's true word in the message!

The confirmation of the word was so strong.

Only God could do this!

Only God knew I was planning on leaving after the session, and that the defendants did everything to destroy me within the justice system. I trusted I had completed the research and investigation of the case as it unfolded within the court. But, it was not 'completed' in my head or in my heart! I had not forgiven the long list of them, and I had not asked God to forgive them or to help me forgive me!

The word blessed me, and knowing it was so special to me it blessed her, also. And then, I had to begin the process of forgiving each of them and forgiving me.

In this moment, I clearly knew a key reason why God wanted me to be at the women's conference.

How special I felt – well, it was equal to how embarrassed I felt – how many 'God meetings, God plans' had I missed up to this point in my life due to my limited human plans?

In this moment, I finally realized that my attendance at the meeting had nothing to do with me being prepared for anything, or for me to do anything for anyone.

God merely asked me to go, to attend.

God kept it simple!

I just have to show up! God had a plan that He announced before I arrived, to the hearts of other saints and not just to me. Then, he confirmed it to me.

So, even though I was 'once again' questioning the wisdom of God, I knew 'once again' that we serve an awesome God, a God who will bless us 'in spite of ourselves'.

THANK GOD!

Wow, my mind was flooded as I started to think about how many times I had **'missed my blessing'** because I was so busy living my **'human limited plan'** that I had personally put into place while not living in alignment with God's plan for my life.

Now, you would think that I realized this truth by this time. However, it is important to remember I'm still in training and thank God I will be in training for the rest of my life!

It is very clear to me that I have a 'human" limited mind and perspective and I have to constantly remind myself to check all steps with the Holy Spirit!

And on that day, I learned how deeply I needed to forgive and ask God to forgive the people but, it required more training for God to help me realize the person I rarely, OK almost never forgive ... is me.

How long would I have continued questioning God's plan by repeating what the 'well meaning' Christian friends were asking me to remember, **"How can you go forth in the world and say you represent God, especially since you are not:**

1. a bible scholar,

2. trained, as an evangelist or bible teacher,

3. mentored by a bible scholar for many years,

4. a pastor,

5. have the proper credentials from accredited Christian universities,

6. an established ministry, with a government nonprofit structure and a board of directors already in place,

7. able to go forth and help others, when your own life is a mess?"

What are we doing to each other? LORD reign! What are we saying about the ministries God is birthing around the world? LORD reign! Do we analyze the person or the ministry based upon our limited human opinions or do we check with the Holy Spirit and only share what God says about the person and the ministry work they are doing?

Henrietta Mears *"Not your responsibility, but your response to God's ability counts. Live the Gospel first! Tell about it afterward! What you are is God's gift to you. What you can become is your gift to Him."*

Henry Clay Trumbull *"Not prayer without faith, nor faith without prayer, but prayer in faith, is the cost of spiritual gifts and graces."*

Chapter 10 Is Your Answer Yes?

Well, God was training me and sending me forth, and God is training each of us, exactly as we are to continue to train each other as Jesus confirmed we are to do in:

Matthew 28:19. *Therefore, go and make disciples of all nations, baptizing them in the name of the Father, and of the Son, and of the Holy Spirit, and teaching them to obey everything I have commanded you. And surely I am with you always, to the very end of the age.*

So, as we STAND firm, together in this moment, are we still open to God's training program? Are we able to persevere & listen to God's whispers, so we do not 'miss' what God has 'in store' for us?

1 Corinthians 2:9. However, as it is written: *"No eye has seen, no ear has heard, no mind has conceived what God has ('in store') prepared for those who love Him"*

For months, not once did I say, ***"YES…God I will go…you can send me, as you know everything about me, and if you think that I can be of service to You…to fulfill upon Your plan … then, I will go…send me … whether it is across the street to help a neighbor, across the aisle or in a different pew at church, if you say 'help them' I will not question your wisdom."***

Not once!

Clearly that would have been the smart response. However, I was so 'world success plan trained' and the body of Christ asks those questions first, so I was truly giving credit to 'the world' for my success and wanting to be approved, and not aligned with God.

I actually let everyone around me 'in the world' tell me God was wrong. So, I was merely repeating to God the "***I'm not ready, yet"*** claims of the 'well meaning' Christians in my life!

So, in this moment, again, I was forgetting, again, God has a purpose and a plan, and in spite of my human-ness, God still wanted to deal with me, exactly as he found me, and to realize He was OK with me while I was still in my human limited condition!

Who would have guessed? God has a great sense of humor to NOT forsake us and to continue to work with us until we comprehend God's plan.

We do serve an awesome God!

Now, finally, I was beginning to realize how often each day I actually questioned God's wisdom in my own words, thoughts and deeds, and I was not apologizing for thinking I knew what I should do and when and how, on my own. So, I had a lot of things to pray about regarding how I was 'walking a la Sheila through my life'.

My prayers shifted from a laundry list of questions: ***"What is happening with this problem? Have you taken care of it, yet, God? I do not see what you are doing, yet, God!"*** to one form of communication: ***"Praise you Lord. Thank you Christ and for the Holy Spirit guiding me, showing me -- what you planned for us to do today, Lord – it was great. Thank you for carrying me when I needed it and not giving up on me when you needed me to stretch my level of understanding, again, to comprehend Your wisdom. Thank you LORD!"***

It is a good thing God has a lot of patience & a sense of humor in dealing with humans! What a process -- to just be with God in prayer, sharing how I have been blessed and how His people are being blessed. It took a long time, but I finally woke up! I'm not perfected yet. But, life is good because I'm still here and God is still talking to me!

Psalm 22:2-4. *O My God, I cry in the daytime, but You do not hear, and in the night season, and am not silent. 3 But You are holy, enthroned in the praises of Israel. 4 Our fathers trusted in You. They trusted, and You delivered them.*

There is nothing that compares! The sad part is, it took years of being trained by the world to follow the world's success plan, and for some reason I was holding on to all of the 'world based plans' that take years to develop to a worthy level and not grabbing on to God's plan...which God can change in the blink of an eye!

Miraculous moments!

2 Corinthians 13:11 and 14. *Finally, brethren, farewell. Become complete. Be of good comfort, be of one mind, live in peace; and the God of love and peace will be with you.* [14] *The grace of the Lord Jesus Christ, and the love of God, and the communion of the Holy Spirit be with you all. Amen.*

Hebrews 13: 7 + *Remember your leaders who spoke the word of God to you. Consider the outcome of their way of life and imitate their faith. Jesus Christ is the same yesterday and today and forever."*

May we seek leadership who already live the way of life we want to imitate. In the meantime, God can free our mind of 'worry' while we begin to understand God's plan for our lives.

When we agree to listen to God more, we will be able to listen so deeply that we hear God even when He whispers!

When I understood this 'error' in my life, by realizing I needed to listen more, to express my faith more and to focus upon the blessings in my life more and more and more, until I could hear God always, especially when He whispers ... that is when God could finally take me on a major 'Faith Walk'.

Often, while God has taken me around the world and when I'm praying with the people, God whispers in my ear, ***"Ask them to listen for My voice, even when I whisper."***

Each time, the recipient of this prayer is so deeply blessed they cry (and often sob; dry cleaning bill for shoulders of my suits is the biggest item for God to handle upon my return) because they realize how deeply God loves us…each of us who hear His message after we cry out to Him to hear His voice!

So, I join with you in this moment that thousands of angels will be dispatched on your behalf, for God knows your pleas, your cries, and the power in fellowshipping and praying two or more together, so cry out and know I am with you in your cries for God to lift you up and out of whatever situation you are finding yourself in, in this moment! To God be the glory!

If I had not experienced the serious circumstances which provided the time and availability to go, I may have missed hearing God's words in response to my own requests, because I would have gone based upon my knowledge and leaned upon my own understanding. I could have missed God's plan for my life, completely. As you can tell by now, I was headed there! God confirmed to me, *"…you stop the flow of my words, each time you resist My purpose and plan for your life."* In the next moment, it felt like God was hugging me and we both cried!

God is so loving, and so right! His quick response was deep! Finally, I said, **"OK, I get the concept, let the one who has not sinned cast the first stone."** Progress!!!

And, what has happened to us as the church today, the body of Christ? What are we doing beyond our own personal plan for the future God has 'laid out' before us, anything? What part of our day is set aside for Kingdom business to be fulfilled? Are we even doing Kingdom business? Are we beginning our day with the process of tithing our time? God is not focused upon 'a tithe of the money' only, while it is part of the process to tithe of our blessings, our increase – God wants a tithe of us, a tithe of all we are ... a tithe of all! Again, ***God's Storehouse Principle:*** This is the message God has given to me, again and again, as I have traveled with him, for we are 'in the church' perhaps, but we are not operating individually 'as the church' based upon the Prophets and Apostles, with Christ as the Chief Cornerstone!

Ephesians 2:20: (church) built on the foundation of the apostles and prophets, with Christ Jesus himself as the **chief cornerstone**.

God's desire is for us experience His blessings when we align with His word and will:

1 Corinthians 2:9. Wisdom From the Spirit. ...it is written: *"No eye has seen, no ear has heard, no mind has conceived what God has ("in store") prepared for those who love him"*

Do we know why we are here? Do we comprehend why God needs each of us to be here? Are we listening to what God is saying, and to what God is asking us to do? And, when we hear His plan, do we say YES or NO?

When we finally say YES, then, the action steps unfold, and yet, we can spend weeks and months questioning our ability to fulfill upon God's plan. And, I trust I'm not alone in this process! Am I right? But, if I can save (or shave) a week or a month or a year or two off waiting for you to experience God's blessed plans for you – so you can experience more, today, then I am honored!

There was so much work to do, and it amazed me that God wanted me to help. I was not a bible scholar, and I'm still not a bible scholar. So, how could I help? What are we capable of? Are we not His chosen and able to do much?

It was amazing to see what God could do through me, when I let God be in control. God confirmed that if I will go in His name, when I open my mouth...He will fill it! And, God did as he promises in **Luke 21:15** *"For I will give you words and wisdom that none of your adversaries will be able to resist or contradict."* I pray He always fills my mouth with His words, and I pray we stand together as we stand in awe each time He speaks through us to the people in our lives, the people in our family and those we know, and the people God introduces us to across the street, in the local stores, and around the world!

Oh yes, back to the women's conference...since God had more than one message waiting for me! When I arrived the last morning, I was already in a long line of people to thank the speaker ... a blessing, and an addition to my schedule, since I was going to leave after the afternoon session the day before ... but, due to God's powerful message, I stayed.

Another God Connection and Introduction

Little did I know how important it was going to be for me to meet the speaker. To me, it was important to let her know she is a wonderful speaker and she has blessed my life. The people she was talking to were going to meet with her again after the session, so they all 'parted the walkway' to let me walk up to her and thank her, Bobbye Byerly, the AGLOW National President.

She immediately took my hands and prayed with me, telling me about my life and confirming God's plan for these days, and she invited me to a church where she would be speaking that evening, and all of this took place in less than a couple of minutes.

At the same time, she was handing me her personal card, while telling me when I visit her town, I will stay with her at her home... her husband will makedinner for us and, we both smiled. Personally, I was laughing inside. I had not been to 'her town' (Colorado Springs) since my Senior skip day, which was clearly a few years ago!

She was prompted by the Holy Spirit to make the invitation, which was confirmed only by God as she did not recall the exact words when I talked with her at the church a few hours later.

We still laugh about this each time we get together, as we have become special friends – starting with the prompting of the Holy Spirit that day, and she did not even remember saying that I would be in her home, staying with her or that her husband would make an amazing meal for us while she was picking me up from the airport, when she proclaimed what the Holy Spirit placed upon her heart, announcing the plan before it is known by us. God is good!

That evening, God's plan was announced to her as she prayed with me. She confirmed I was to go to a men's ministry (the three years of Jonah and the whale reminders), and I would know that

God had ordained the trip prior to the day it unfolded. God's promise resulted in blessing me with time in her home, spending days with the men's ministry (the next assignment), exactly **three weeks** after the women's conference.

God knew and announced to us, before it unfolded! We do serve an awesome God!

While I was getting ready to leave…since I was the last car in the parking lot after the conference, it was clear … I do know that I know how dearly I was blessed to be there and to savor each moment of what God wanted to do with me and for me.

Another God Connection and Introduction

Then, due to the invitation from Bobbye Byerly and the AGLOW host pastor, I attended the service at the pastor's local church to hear Bobbye again. And, I met several of the women from the conference and their families who are still close friends today.

At the end of the service, many of the women from the conference were standing in line waiting for prayer. God prompted me to bring forward a woman who was not at the conference.

The Holy Spirit was connecting the two of us, prior to the time when the Lord would confirm His next plans in my life through her. Amazing! The group parted so my new friend could pray with Bobbye. Then God blessed me with one more prayer from my new, dear sister in Christ whom I value sharing time with each time God brings us together one more time! Within the prayer, God confirmed even more about the next steps for me to accept His request to go the men's ministry, and once again I knew that God had a plan that was beyond my comprehension and 'out of my control'. Training was speeding up. We do serve an awesome God!

Lord be with me, always, send me where You need me to be in the world, protected by the blood of my Savior, Jesus Christ, while I remain aligned with Your will, so Your purpose and plan for my life will be fulfilled. Amen.

Smith Wigglesworth *"We become supernatural by the power of God. We find this power working through every part of our being."*

Kathryn Kuhlman *"Today, Jesus stands ready to hear your cry and to answer prayer for you. He is interested in every detail of your life. He knows you better than you know yourself and is touched with the feeling of your infirmities and your needs. It is my prayer that even now Jesus shall make His Person and Presence a reality to you and give you His faith, and complete confidence in His power and love and promises - and the desire of your heart."*

Habakkuk 2:3 *Faith in God includes Faith in his timing*

Benny Hinn *"I walk in the realm of the supernatural."*

Psalm 27:1 *The Lord is my light and my salvation; Whom shall I fear? The Lord is the strength of my life; Of whom shall I be afraid?*

Chapter 11 Launched to a Men's Ministry

For several months in fact, for three years while I resisted God's invitation to go with God anywhere, especially since God had prompted me to pray fervently for a men's ministry. I did not know any details beyond the fact the founder of the ministry was well known and I was acquainted with his book. I did not know the ministry staff or team, or the men who were attending the conferences around the country with this ministry.

Each day I resisted this 'plan', since I am clearly not a man, as I shared previously, and yet, the funny part is, God clearly knew this before He asked me to go. God's response to each man's name was clear: *"Not this time. I am asking you to go."*

An extra interesting fact: God told the woman who spoke at the women's conference, Bobbye Byerly, National President of

AGLOW and on the staff of the new World Prayer Center in Colorado Springs, Colorado, that I was being asked to go to the men's ministry before I shared it with her.

When I asked her about the ministry, she confirmed she knew of the ministry.

When I asked her who she thought should go, she responded, **"I think God knew who to send when He asked you."** Then, when we realized God was so clear and quick in the confirmation, we both looked at each other and laughed!

God did a quick work. This happened as part of the conversation within the two minutes while we prayed together during the women's conference. I told her that I have been praying and I will continue to pray for the men's ministry, and this is when she responded while handing me her card, ***"...when you come, you will stay in our home..."*** Her card was God's confirmation since the woman lives in the same area of the country as the headquarters for the men's ministry.

To seek further confirmation, I asked if she knew any of the people praying for the ministry. She provided the phone number for the leader of the prayer team plus she introduced me to the prayer team through a conference call. The call was so powerful.

Then, the prayer team leaders arranged for the prayer team to pray over my name, asking God to reveal who I am per the scriptures. God provided a specific scripture for each of the seven members / couples of the prayer team. God confirmed the assignment so the team leader called to say I needed to be there in seven days. Then, the seven scriptures were shared. When I looked up the scriptures, they were a perfect outline of the chronological history of my life!

This was a surprise to me.

However, the prayer team received additional confirmations that I should meet and pray with them before I meet with the ministry staff. So, God arranged the time and the ticket for me to accept the flight schedule to be with the ministry in seven days.

God provided the flight. Bobbye picked me up at the airport while her husband made a special dinner for us, exactly as God stated when we prayed and she handed me her card. Plus, I was a guest in their home that evening. We serve an awesome God!

There was more training for God to do with me, before I arrived.

A long time friend called to tell me she was thinking about me and then, when she was praying about me she was prompted to call me and remind me about the **"Three days of Jonah in the whale."** She asked if I knew what God wanted me to know about the story of Jonah.

This call gave me the opportunity to describe God's training program with her, also. She was amazed and agreed to pray me through this 'Faith Walk' to Colorado. This was a new term for me, but, she said, *"You are going on a faith walk with God, and that is not always an easy journey, so extra prayers will be added to*

my schedule each day, until you are back and you can tell me the glorious details about what God does through you, when you are in their midst!"

Then, God asked a long time prayer partner, a woman I had not seen in months, to call me and ask me if God was asking me to travel to a city, as she was sure God had prompted her to call me and ask me about ***"The three days of Jonah in the whale."***

Again, I was given the opportunity to share my testimony of the training program God was orchestrating in my life. She was in tears, because she thought I was going to be stuck vs. being launched. She congratulated me about my chance to be launched, a.k.a., ***"getting out of my whale experience."***

Then, exactly three days before the flight to the men's ministry, at the exact time in the morning as the flight departure time, a woman I did not know very well, the woman I walked down the aisle with for prayer on Sunday evening three weeks ago called the pastor for my personal phone number. It was a surprise since I did not know the woman beyond our walk down the church aisle. However, she told me that since she met me at the church, God had repeatedly prompted her to pray for me.

She went on to say that she had called the pastor and told him about having a vision and seeing me in the vision. It was so vivid it caused her to wake up her husband in the middle of the night to tell him the details so she would not forget. The pastor received immediate confirmation from God & told her to keep him up to date about what God is doing in our lives in these days!

The woman told me God shared a vision with her about the tree of life and the leaf that was being handed to me. She was told it was <u>the leaf of relationship and reconciliation, I am here to unite the people, the body of Christ, for God's purpose to be fulfilled,</u> and she did not know why she was seeing me in the vision until she heard the last words God said, ***"…be sure to tell Sheila about my message, to confirm my plan for her, and remind Sheila about 'the three days of Jonah in the whale.' She will understand."***

Well, it was clear to me, and it had been confirmed by many prayer partners and pastors, God was doing more than delivering a message. God was also asking me to share my 'denominational card carrying' traits with the people in my life. I can relate to the people who are or were 'fellow pew warmers', the faithful ones who keep coming back to the church because they want a deep relationship with God and they hope it will happen this time or the next time we sit in the pew. I identified with everything the woman shared.

Lord, help us be in a close relationship with you and with each other, so the reconciliation of the body of Christ will be evident in our generation and be passed on to the third and fourth generations.

The reason why God shared the vision of the tree of life is to confirm to me that God has given her the words to share with me. We both laughed when God confirmed I was to share the testimony of who I am and what I am to do when she said, ***"…be sure to***

remind Sheila about the 'three days of Jonah in the whale,' and she will understand." She was deeply blessed to hear the many experiences and to hear my testimony. She told her husband and we spent extra time together during the three days before my flight to the men's ministry.

She arranged with her husband to meet with me in Dallas during my brief lay-over of my return flight, as they would be back in their Dallas, Texas home by the time I returned from the men's ministry. They requested prayer for their friend, John Willison. Trusting you are seeing how amazing it is to faith walk with God when He divinely orchestrates all of the details!

God has More to Reveal Before the Flight

While I was packing on Sunday night for the Monday morning flight, God prompted me to go back to church and attend the evening service. Since I was at the church in the morning and I was flying out the next morning, sorry to say this but, I still resisted.

To make a long story of resistance short, you only need to know I was a little late for the service.

While I was looking for a seat, the praise team music was ending as the pastor took the microphone, *"...the sermon is not going to be about the three days of Jonah in the whale tonight. You can look up the story and read it after the service. However, someone needs to hear the truth about the story tonight, so I do have a trivia question for you. Do you know how Jonah got out of the whale?"*

Well, I was smiling and softly whispering the same words (to myself) I thought I heard many people whispering, *"...he accepted the assignment."*

And, I knew then, I'm here to hear this message since I'm accepting the assignment.

Clearly, I hope I'm out of the whale… and yet, I did not realize my mouth was open and the words actually came out of me: *"…since I know the story…"* while I was walking toward an open seat.

The pastor stated, *"You may think you know the story. You are probably thinking you know it because you know Jonah accepted the assignment. However, the main point is often missed. The fact is God could only have asked Jonah to go on the assignment <u>after</u> Jonah became grateful for all of the experiences in his life, the training which led up to this point in his life so God knew that Jonah was ready to go on the assignment. So, are you grateful for all of your experiences?"*

Wow. Stunned. Clearly, I was stopped in my tracks.

Tears flowed.

I am supposed to be grateful for all of the experiences that led up to this assignment, God?

I'm to be grateful for the many attacks, all of the misunderstandings … for all that has happened to me?

Wow. It took me a few extra moments to realize I needed to pray through each of the attacks and be sure all was forgiven to be an empty and open vessel, so God and the Holy Spirit could fill me to over flowing, to be useful for God's purposes while I am on assignment!

God's prompting to be at the church service was perfect, and the word shared meant I had a lot of work to do to be sure I was ready for this assignment, way beyond just packing my bags!

When I prayed that night, I apologized since God had asked me first...before so many others, and I was glad to accept the assignment. Again, when I thanked God and yet, still felt 'unworthy' God responded, *"Remember, I asked them, and they told me NO."* Before I could say thank you for sending me, God continued, *"... as often as you responded NO to me, when your life was so busy with your busy-ness and your plans...you missed out on the blessings I had 'in store' for you, to do Kingdom business..."* as tears flowed & flowed! Thank God this training process is 'on-going' and it has no deadline or expiration date!

Flight to the Men's Ministry

Prayers with the prayer team leaders were powerful. I was reviewing the notes on the flight. I wanted to be as open as I could be to do Kingdom business every moment we would have to share together. I prayed each word would support the efforts of the prayer team and the ministry leaders, God's words He wanted me to share which would confirm the reasons God wanted us to meet together with the men's ministry.

The ministry was in need of restructuring even though they had just restructured. God provided the specific facts only God would know.

God revealed specific changes required to cause the ministry to flow again, so the time together led to additional meetings and hours of prayer sessions.

Alignment of Personal Time within God's Plan

God's plan matched with the wedding plans of a long time friend.

She was engaged and had recently, coincidentally, moved to the same city as the men's ministry.

So, this timing was perfect!

We spent time together. We traveled to and from the wedding together, so I was able to provide the prayers for the new couple on their wedding day!

Travel arrangements to her wedding were not possible…prior to God's flight being scheduled to the exact location…so we had decided I would not be at her wedding, a 'fact' that was confirmed just a few days prior to God arranging the flight to the men's ministry!

God has amazing timing, and his orchestration of travel arrangements causes me to stand in awe!

While I was at the wedding, the prayer team was meeting with the leadership of the ministry. After the wedding, I returned to meet once again with the prayer team.

Then, we met with the key leaders and staff members of the men's ministry.

Meeting with Staff of the Men's Ministry

God showed me a vision. The vision confirmed God gave the ministry to a man God placed in the leadership role, and yet, he was OK with a new plan of stepping back and letting the man with the world plan proceed instead of re-aligning the team with God's vision and stepping into the future of the ministry.

God confirmed a man with a world plan was influencing the ministry man who brought this plan to the leader, so the changes to align with the world plan were going forward and causing the current problems experienced by the ministry. The leader needed to be re-established as the leader and the team needed to seek God's guidance on the next steps.

The people were not known to me and the request for God to confirm that the words shared had blessed the men was responded to with the comment of the key pastor. As he was excusing himself from our meeting to go to another meeting, he took my hand between his hands and said, *"Some day, just one time in my life, may our Lord introduce me to someone as He has just introduced you to me."*

The message was directed to him and it was specific for him.

Tears flowed. He was mightily blessed!

The team presented me with Bill McCartney's book, **Sold Out.**

When he was in San Diego for a meeting, since Bishop George McKinney is or was the Chaplin for Promise Keepers, I was invited to attend the meeting.

Since I was an 'add on' to the meeting, I felt it was not right for me to make a personal request for Bill to autograph the book. So, I was whispering to Bishop to see if he would take the book with him since the men were going to lunch and on to the airport. I hoped if they had a chance to talk for a moment Bishop could ask Bill to autograph my book.

He overheard my soft whispers, turned and walked toward us saying, **"So, you want your Bishop do your bidding?"** He was beaming. I was embarrassed.

He autographed the book and motioned to the photographer to take a photo of us which was included within an article in the local newspaper. God is so good!

Back to what God's word did for the men's ministry. Due to my resistance in accepting the assignment, aka three years of delaying God's schedule, the ministry had laid off a lot of people.

The word God gave to them because I accepted the assignment provided the exact confirmation needed for the team to re-structure the ministry per God's plans within days. Within weeks, the ministry was flourishing once again.

It was my thought, my logical process a la Sheila, to want to stay in touch or at least request to know how I can assist them further.

Why? I'm a business coach. It's what I relied upon in the past, aka, how I rolled in business in the world.

However, God's assignments are only what God ordains and orchestrates and not one more ounce added, aka 'no leaven' as Jesus warned the disciples to watch their words and make sure they only deliver the word and they do not add to the word.

It was new to me that I was done as soon as the word of the Lord was delivered. God's work and God's schedule and timing were brand new to me.

Thank God the Holy Spirit confirmed the assignment was complete:

1. the word was delivered,
2. the word was acted upon, so there is nothing else to do as God's assignment was complete.

More training was required. I'm so used to the 'roll up the sleeves and get busy doing the work.'

God constantly shifts my thinking within his daily training plans with me! Plus, God knew another assignment was waiting for me during what I thought would merely be a brief lay-over in Dallas on my way back to California.

Lord be with me, always, send me where you need me to be in the world, protected by the blood of my Savior, Jesus Christ, while I remain aligned with your will, so your purpose and plan for my life will be fulfilled. Amen.

Newspaper Photograph
Bill McCartney with Sheila Holm
After he autographed *Sold Out*

Kathryn Kuhlman "Remember something, God never permitted a difficulty to come into our life without also giving us the ability to handle it. God has provided us with every faculty. He has given us the power that we need for living victoriously. It is a fact that everyone of us down deep has what it takes to successfully meet whatever life brings."

Martin Luther *"Faith is permitting ourselves to be seized by the things that we do not see ... Faith is a living and unshakable confidence, a belief in the grace of God so assured that a man would die a thousand deaths for its sake."*

Chapter 12 Texas and Beyond in a Small Plane, Yikes!

The couple who received the vision, the new prayer partners who have a home in California and in Dallas, met me at the Dallas-Fort Worth airport. <u>Humor Insert</u>: Immediately after the pilot announced we were to prepare for landing, the wife of the couple sitting behind me asked her husband: *Why don't they just call it the Dallas or Forth Worth airport?* His response: *It's probably the same reason why our airport is Minneapolis-St. Paul.* Without hesitation, his wife said: *We have a reason! The Catholics are on the St. Paul side and the Protestants are on the Minneapolis side.*

My new friends had arranged for a time of prayer with their friend, John Willison, during a special lunch at their favorite restaurant. As soon as we shared a quick meal, especially since

God confirmed the prayers required privacy, we followed John's vehicle to a peaceful suburb to continue the prayers at his home.

John was hosting a house guest involved in a Pastor's conference, an amazing singer and man of God, Earl Harrigan. The prayers were intense. Earl heard the depth of the message and linked the details to what could unfold for John in the natural. The details caused all of us to be in awe of what God does when we gather together.

Earl was getting ready to sing that evening at Pastor Nichol's church for the Pastor's Conference.

When Earl realized I had not heard him sing before, he simply stated, *"...you will be there tonight."*

"No" was my quick reply, while I laughed and told him that time was tight for me to be at the airport, since the flight was scheduled to leave before he would be singing at the conference.

Without taking much of a breath, I went on to say that I was sorry I was leaving, however, I would enjoy hearing him sing someday.

He looked at me again and said, *"God knows the plan...you will be there tonight...it is part of God's plan."*

When I confirmed again it would not be possible, since I am scheduled to return home on the next flight he asked, *"What is scheduled at home that would keep you from attending the meeting?"*

When I started talking about the $75 cost to change the flight schedule and I went on a bit about not being sure the airline would allow me to change the flight, he asked me to call the airlines. Then, he told John to pay the fee because the confirmation of God's word in the prayers is worth at least that much.

Everyone laughed, while Earl stated again that I was going to be staying in Texas a while, and that I was *"...not going home anytime soon."*

As I was confirming the flight change with the airline representative on the phone, and then, the customer service employee, the staff confirmed they are in the Dallas office so they decided to attend the meeting that evening, also.

At this point, John reached into his pocket and handed me a $100 bill.

Everyone laughed, again!

This change in schedule needed to be confirmed with the couple I would be staying with as this meant that I would be staying in the home of a couple I was just getting to know, and they had not opened their home to guests or even their family members before, so we were all 'in training' while God was revealing His plans in the moment, and not one moment sooner!

They said they were in agreement with what God is doing, and then, we decided to share a quick meal before the evening meeting.

The heavy traffic caused us to be a few minutes late for the meeting.

As we entered the conference hall, a couple of young men were standing a few feet in front of us.

As I started to walk past them, one of them said, *"Ma'am please pray for us."*

Since we were late and the meeting was part of a pastor's conference, I quickly told the young men a pastor from the conference would probably pray with them, as I'm not a pastor and I do not have authority ... but, the young man interrupted and looked at me again as he said, *"God told me as soon as you came in the door that you would pray with us."*

Reassuring him that I would be glad to pray with him, however I needed to ask a pastor to join us, since I was not from the area and I did not have any authority to pray with them at the conference. Then, I excused myself to enter the conference hall and find a pastor, while my new hosts remained with the boys.

As I entered the auditorium, a man who sang at a Rodney Howard-Browne meeting in San Diego a few weeks before, Big John Hall, was walking toward the aisle as he stated in his deep voice, *"What are you doing in my hometown?"*

Before I could comprehend his question, he said, *"You are from San Diego."*

OK. I was really shocked, now.

The Rodney Howard-Browne meeting I attended in San Diego was in a packed auditorium. I knew Big John Hall from years of singing with **The Gaithers** but I was not introduced to him 'in the natural' during the Rodney Howard-Browne meeting.

Wow. He could tell I was surprised, and evidently 'speechless,' as he stated, **"God is glad you are here and so am I."**

All I could do is thank him, as I was still shocked that he recognized me, and that he knew I was from San Diego.

The timing was perfect, however, as I needed to find a pastor and I trusted he knew the pastors in the conference.

When I asked him to refer a pastor, he asked who had invited me.

As I searched the room, I pointed to the singer I had just met, Earl Harrigan. I told him that I was invited by Earl moments before the meeting, as I pointed to Earl in the front row. Then, Big John Hall told me to go to the side door and motion to Earl. He smiled as he told me to ask Earl to refer me to a pastor.

As I motioned to Earl, he walked to the side door. He knew I was urgently requesting some assistance, so I quickly shared the request of the two young men and that I needed to involve a pastor with authority as I do not have authority in this setting. Earl started to walk briskly to the front entrance where the boys were waiting.

Big John Hall knew what I did not, Earl is a pastor. Earl agreed to pray with me. I was relieved for a moment, but then he said, **"You will be praying for the young men, because they already know that God sent you here to pray with them."**

We prayed with the young men, while one stated he had been indoctrinated into Satanism eight years before and the other young man was a follower of Satan for ten years, and the friend had introduced him into Satanism.

Then he stated they had received prayer from one of the pastors earlier in the day. They asked Jesus Christ to be their Savior, but, when they left the conference hall they experienced severe headaches.

Immediately, it was clear the men were blessed to be powerfully taken into the anointing of and empowered by the Holy Spirit. It was perfect for me, because God took over and gave each of them exactly what they needed.

God continued to bless them, each time they tried to get up … again & again.

We sat with them, shared God's words with them, informed them of the basic battle we are all in 'in the world' between the powers of Satan and the power and authority of Jesus Christ. Their smiles made it obvious that we had encouraged them as their countenance changed right before our eyes!

Then, as we were preparing to enter the conference hall, the young men asked, *"Ma'am we want to know where you are from, and we want to know how God sent you to us."*

As I started to say, *"I'm from San Diego…God has extended my stay"* Earl stated, *"…and God is confirming again why she is here now, and she is not going to be home again anytime soon."*

The couple joined us as we all entered the conference hall

We realized now that we had missed the song Earl was singing at the opening of the meeting. However, we laughed again since we all realized God's timing for us was perfect, again!

Another Opportunity to Serve

Later in the week, we attended an evening service of a local church to finally hear our new Christian friend, Earl Harrigan, sing. Earl also included me with the prayer team after the service.

A woman requested prayers, and her eyes were covered so that she was not able to see clearly.

I immediately began praying for her soul.

My friends came forward as they were concerned because I was dripping wet while praying.

I told them that I felt I was praying for the woman's soul as she was not able to gain release…Earl took my hand and said, **"The Lord releases her and He releases you…"** and the couple noticed that the heat, the sweating, the curling of my hair stopped 'in that moment' and the woman was also released.

Another Opportunity to Serve

On Sunday, we attended the service where Earl was singing and preaching.

It was a fabulous service.

After the service, Earl called me forward again to minister to the members coming forward and asking for prayer.

A woman came forward. The Lord healed her internal problems as she coughed (into a couple of boxes of Kleenex) until the 'contents' were released.

After the service, she told the pastor and Earl that she had experienced numerous stomach surgeries, including follow-up surgeries to remove the scar tissue. She felt better after the Lord released the 'contents' of what she was coughing up. She wanted them to know how powerful the prayers were for her life.

Earl blessed me by saying, **"Whenever you are in the same town I am in, we will be doing ministry work together."**

God's training was continuing and again I had to stand in awe as God revealed His plan for each person receiving prayers.

A Women's Conference in Arkansas

The original man I prayed for when I arrived, John, called my host and hostess and stated that God wanted me to be at a women's conference in Arkansas. Before they explained the details, I was still thinking no while I heard my voice saying, ***YES.***

I had no idea how I would be able to get to Arkansas but, they stated John is a private pilot and he has offered to fly me to Arkansas.

The host couple needed to leave for a conference, so they told me that it was up to me if I thought I should go home or stay in a hotel until the end of the week.

I told them, without hesitation, that I would make arrangements to stay in the area and attend the conference.

Arrangements were made (without credit cards or funds) to be at a local hotel. After I checked in, a call confirmed I would be attending a taping of a Christian TV show that evening.

After the show, I was taken to dinner and the time was getting a bit late, so I stated that I needed to get some rest before the flight the next day.

When we returned to the hotel, before saying good-night, the host for the evening stated an apology was in order as God had asked him to give me $100. He was not sure what the funds were for. However, after dinner, God confirmed again that he was supposed to give me $100.

The next morning, I was checking out a half hour before the 'pilot' was picking me up to go to Arkansas. I asked the clerk how much the Hotel bill was, including the taxes, and the bill was $103 and change. God had provided for the bill to be paid in full! Again, we do serve an awesome God.

Since the pilot, John, was hosting Earl, the two of them picked me up and we were heading to Arkansas. I felt sorry for them, as we pre-checked the plane. I was going to a women's conference and they were arranging a fishing trip with a guide, staying at a cabin in Northern Arkansas. I quickly shared 'kits' for them, small bottles of my favorite waterless soap and items I hoped would help them!

To my surprise, I was staying in youth camp cabins and the 'guys' were staying in a four star resort! The gift shop of their cabin resort was bigger than one of our cabins! Ah, the sense of humor our God has when we are on assignment!

Holy Spirit Evident to Baby
Listening to an Anointed Song

The first night, I was the only person staying in the cabins.

The 'on site' Manager stopped by and offered to let me use her CD player, to listen to the new **Shout!** CD of my new library for Earl Harrigan's music. We all enjoyed the music, and especially the song: **Walk on the Water.**

Then, she invited me to her home. The song actually caused her granddaughter, a few months old, to raise her arms and sing praises to the Lord.

The woman was so surprised about what she heard while she was in the other room with her grandson that she came back into the room to find out what was causing her granddaughter to sing.

So, I told her to change the CD player to the song before this song…the baby had no reaction…then, when she played the same song, **Walk On the Water** her granddaughter raised her hands and started to sing, again…we were blessed to realize her granddaughter's reaction.

We enjoyed our evening together. The most difficult part of the conference … keeping it a secret that the women were going to meet my new Christian friends, John and Earl, on Saturday

The first three women arriving at the conference became my close confidants.

I told them I was 'just attending,' however the Holy Spirit confirmed to them that I had another assignment, so we immediately became close prayer partners, asking God to reveal the truth during the next few days together.

Women Blessed by John Willison's Testimony and Earl Harrigan Singing *Amazing Grace*

John & Earl returned on Saturday, surprising the women with a special video of John's testimony.

When the video reached the point where Earl sings ***Amazing Grace***, Earl came down the aisle singing the song.

Then, while the story was shared about the granddaughter and her reaction to: ***Walk on the Water***, the audio tapes and CD's sold out in less than 10 minutes.

After confirming they were going to pick me up at the end of the day on Sunday, John and Earl flew through the middle of a storm on their way to Oklahoma. That's right, God actually parted the clouds for them to fly through the storm without turbulence.

A Time of Prayer and Healing Relationships

The leader asked me to share part of my testimony and it deeply touched the women. They requested prayers after the session. In fact, the prayer line was longer than the dinner line that evening!

Three marriages were reconciled due to the prayers, and I was aware I was blessed by God for merely being there.

God knew! Two women were getting divorced the next week.

They called their husbands immediately after our prayers. Their husbands agreed to pick them up at the end of the conference after they said they noticed something different when they spoke to their wives...it is so amazing to realize what God will do 'in the in-between' of our major decisions, when we follow through with a few minor details – keeping it all in prayer!

Oklahoma

Early on Sunday, Earl & John sent a message for me to be ready to leave after the first session.

The Lord had confirmed to the Oklahoma Pastor and his wife, also raised in Nebraska, for me to be with them for both of their Sunday services.

Ministering with my new singer and pastor friend, Earl, and even with and to the local pastor and his wife was an added blessing. The people were so appreciative that I chose to be with them and the Pastor and his wife hosted me at their home.

Blessed, Returning Home

The next day, we flew back to Texas in the small plane [4] and I returned home on the next flight to California. Life has not been the same, since. God had provided unique training in Texas, with special invitations from the first moment I arrived until the moment I departed.

This experience was beyond my ability and expectations expressed by each of us participating within God's plan for these days.

The friendships which were further established together resulted in many blessings. I've been fortunate to spend time with Pastor and singer Earl Harrigan in various parts of the world, since meeting him in Texas and each time it is based upon God's timing and plans for us to come together and share the many blessings in our lives since the last time we were together. More confirmations that we serve an awesome God!

Arizona Prophet, Connection Through Earl Harrigan

God introduced me to a 50 year prophet. After a few attempts to connect, God found the perfect time for us to talk! I called and the prophet asked me to immediately share the word of the Lord. The prophet was in tears while I was sharing a word.

I did not know the prophet or that within the exact moment of my call he had asked God to have someone call and confirm what God wanted him to do, a Christian servant he had not met…and, the call which met his request of God was mine.

When I asked if he had a word for me, he said, *"You know … your job is clear. God is preparing you to go forth for the thousands who have not knelt."*

He invited me to meet with him and some of the leaders of his church. We met and many of the church and business leaders were present. God shared specific words through me for each person in attendance, including a pastor friend of Earl Harrigan. The prophet confirmed each word as soon as it was delivered.

The prophet was so deeply touched, he asked me to share dinner with him and his wife that evening, and to share the platform at his church on Sunday, to pray and minister to the people.

God Changed the Plans to Focus Upon the Overview Assignment

Later that day, the prophet was releasing me from being at his church on Sunday.

I was shocked! Immediately, I cried out to God to know why, and without a moment of hesitation, God responded, *"He was your assignment. You are not his assignment."* So, I prayed and rested.

Then, God arranged for me to be up and ready to leave the hotel at 4 AM, to drive to a different church where God knew I was supposed to attend the Sunday service. After the service, the Lord prompted the Pastor to confirm the specific messages He sent through two prophets prior to this date, *"God is preparing you to go forth for the thousands who have not knelt."*

When I returned home, I asked God what I was to prepare for next. God told me to rest, restore and read the message. Then, I would be prepared.

So, I read and re-read and then studied the scriptures regarding the thousands who had not knelt, and this is what the Bible stated in the next verse, **Romans 11:3.** *"Lord they have killed your prophets and torn down your altars; I am the only one left and they are trying to kill me."*

OK. How can I rest and restore myself realizing they want to kill God's prophets!

Instead of letting me feel sorry for myself, God directed me to 'read on' for God was going to reveal his answer in **Romans 11:4b.** *"I have reserved for myself seven thousand who have not bowed the knee to Baal."*

More to Learn About Jonah

Just when I thought I was doing 'well' in the training program with our LORD, further resistance brought me to my knees when God told me to *"...re-read the book of Jonah."* I was a bit prideful when I told God, *"I know that book"* but, God did not criticize me when he gently replied, *"...you do not know the book of Jonah."*

Not realizing I was acting a bit, OK a lot self-righteous, when I read Chapter 1 and said, *"I know that one"* while God was silent.

I read Chapter 2 and I gave God the same response.

Then, I read Chapter 3 and gave God the same response before I turned the page and started reading Chapter 4. Yikes!

To paraphrase the story, God had provided food and shelter from the vine but, when the sun came out it withered the vine and Jonah was not happy. God's provision was not evident but, God got Jonah's attention by adjusting his head just a few degrees to view the city while reminding Jonah he did not plant or tend to the vine. God provided the vine for him, and God told Jonah, ***"And should I not pity Nineveh, that great city, in which are more than 120,000 persons who cannot discern their right hand and their left – and much livestock?"* Jonah 4:11**.

I was wrong, again.

Jonah had a bigger assignment! God was confirming, again, there is a bigger assignment. I apologized to God and confirmed for the first time, ***"If You are showing me this to confirm You are giving me a bigger assignment, You can send me. I will go."***

Martin Luther *"The whole being of any Christian is faith and love. Faith brings the person to God, love brings the person to people."*

George Mueller *"The beginning of anxiety is the end of faith, and the beginning of true faith is the end of anxiety."*

Psalm 84:11 (the last bible verse George Mueller read to his wife Mary before she passed away) *"The Lord God is a sun and shield, the Lord will give grace and glory, no good thing will he withhold from those who walk uprightly."*

Chapter 13 Sent Down Under

Encourage a Pastor

Dr. John P. Kelly, a well-known conference speaker, founder and overseeing apostle of Antioch Churches and Ministries requested that I visit with and encourage a California pastor.

On my part, there was some resistance and a lot of hesitation about renting another car but, God provided and I met with Pastor Harold Dewberry at En Agape church within 24 hours.

The meeting was quickly interrupted with an emergency phone call, so I offered to excuse myself. But, Pastor Dewberry asked me to remain and pray during the call.

At the conclusion of the call, Pastor Dewberry asked what God was saying so I shared the details, *"...the man is having difficulty standing firm and facing what he needs to face. It seems you may need to be with him, on his soil, standing with him and helping him to learn how to face what he needs to face."*

But, he quickly responded, *"God gave a clear message to you. It sounds like you need to be the one to be with him."*

I asked where the man lived. Pastor Dewberry said, *"He is a pastor in Fiji."* Then, he showed me a map of Fiji and multiple photos of the pastors serving in Fiji, a group of pastors reporting to the senior pastor who called. We prayed about all details God was revealing in this hour.

As I was telling Pastor Dewberry I was only there to be with him, to see how I could serve him, he kept smiling. Then he said, *"I will join you in a day of fasting and prayer tomorrow, and we will meet again on Thursday."*

I smiled, but I was shocked!

God knew but, Pastor Dewberry did not know that I was renting cars and on the day when I rent a car I have to run all errands and return the car! Clearly, I felt God was not involved as I knew I was not prepared to rent a car again on Thursday.

Praying on the return trip home while I was feeling upset, asking God why the meeting was so short? And, I have to be honest I really wanted to know how could the focus on Fiji have been so important that it would overshadow the purpose of the meeting? After all, I was there to encourage the pastor and without realizing I was doing it again – in my limited human mind I trusted we did not have the meeting we were supposed to have as I did not encourage the pastor. I was talking and God was not talking!

The rental agency said a car rental would be possible on Thursday but, I told them not to hold a car yet, because I would have to call them on Thursday morning to confirm.

OK, I was worried. I was not sure how God was going to provide the funds for another rental day by Thursday.

Now, I can laugh about it – because God knew about Thursday, before I drove to the church on Tuesday but, at that time, I was being so humanly minded … I was just not sure!

About 3 PM on Wednesday, I was released from fasting and prayer with God's prompting that I was supposed to offer more time with Pastor Dewberry while meeting with him on Thursday. Since I did not know very much about the pastor, I called a few people who had attended his seminars, to check on the work he conducted in ministry. The work was in New Zealand. Many good reports were shared.

As I continued to pray, God was confirming Australia … nothing about New Zealand. I was not receiving confirmations about Fiji or New Zealand, God only stated Sydney, Australia. I did not know what that meant, yet.

That evening, I was invited to speak at a local church.

Women purchased the Christian scarves I offer wherever I speak. The cash was exactly the amount required for the rental car and gas to meet with Pastor Dewberry.

When I arrived at the church on Thursday morning, the staff members were singing. They were so excited I would be going to Fiji. I told them I was very appreciative of their prayers, but I was not sure I was going to Fiji.

Within moments, Pastor Dewberry motioned for me to enter his office. When he asked what God has confirmed, I stated God confirmed we would be spending more time together today, and in the next few days. I also shared the details I was given by people about his seminars in New Zealand. I confirmed God was not confirming anything about New Zealand or Fiji, God only stated Sydney.

At this point, the pastor interrupted my summary by merely stating, **"Great, this time my seminars are being held in a location above Sydney, Australia."**

Laughter, as though I had just won a lottery, is what I offered (it was God's offering as I was still in shock!) as he stated, **"...we will have time to spend together in Australia, but now we need to pack and prepare since the conference begins on Monday."**

It's Thursday afternoon. The conference begins on Monday. I do not have the money to be in Australia...to get a last minute ticket...ah, the sense of humor our Lord possesses!

When I told Pastor Dewberry I had no way to be in Australia on Monday, he asked what I needed. I told him I would need a ticket. He merely pointed to the office across the hall and said I could call the airlines by using a phone in the extra office.

Lord be with me now! I called an airline that I had a few travel miles 'on the books' with, but, each of the employees stated, ***"It would take a miracle..."*** so, each time with God's help I got a little bit stronger when I responded, ***"...I stand on miracles."***

The airline employee in the management office offered a seat on an early flight on Sunday. The staff of American Airlines and their partner airline Qantas in Los Angeles would like to meet me between the domestic and international flights to find out about this woman who needs an urgent flight to be arranged within three days and they wanted to know what was happening in Australia that God had to arrange for me to be there at the last minute. She confirmed a ticket would be available at their ticketing office in San Diego the next day.

Not having a phone at home, a friend at church offered their cellular phone.

My cousin called the ministry host in Australia. They called me back on the cell phone at 2:15 AM on Sunday, before my 6 AM flight.

Since they did not know me, they wanted me to know that they heard I do not have credit or debit cards so they charged the first night at a Sydney hotel on their credit card but, they trusted I would pay the hotel cash at checkout. Yikes!

I was praying during the call. God was still confirming that I was supposed to go to Australia so, I did not say what I felt I should say, *"I need to cancel."* Instead, as God concluded the call I was saying: *"I look forward to meeting you in Newcastle ..."*

Having no idea how I could pay and yet, I had no time to keep thinking about that because I had more packing to do and only a few minutes before I had to leave for the airport!

God had an answer. He prompted me to go to the Post Office on my way to the airport. To my surprise, a check from a New York bank recognized globally was in the box. So, I was flying to Australia with a New York check, virtually no cash, and only the knowledge that I was supposed to go to Australia by Monday to meet with Pastor Dewberry and be part of a conference.

Sydney, Australia

Upon my arrival in Sydney, I asked the shuttle driver for basic directions and how far the hotel is from the airport as I would need to walk. He was puzzled so I explained about the check. He told me that he could take me to the hotel and wait until I found out if they would cash the check. I told him I did not want to do that if I could not pay him. He said it would be worth it for him to hear how this story turns out.

The check was accepted since it was written on the New York bank of J P Morgan Chase, Manhattan, and the exchange rate to Australian dollars provided the exact amount I needed for the room, a snack (apple), the shuttle that night and again the next morning to return to the airport and meet Pastor Dewberry. The shuttle driver was so amazed he came back for me the next morning even though he was off shift, since he wanted to spend the time hearing more details about what God is doing in my life. He wanted to meet Pastor Dewberry so he would have a complete testimony to share with his family and friends. Plus, he made sure I knew they do not tip people in Australia as he said it is different from America, they are honored to serve. What a concept!

Within moments, Pastor Dewberry made the arrangements and we were on a train headed north to be with the host family in Newcastle, NSW Australia. We do serve an awesome God!

Seven days in Australia resulted in being extended seven times, to seven weeks.

The first day set the stage for the entire seven weeks.

A pastor picked me up from the conference center. We were headed to lunch. He asked a few questions and then, he placed a few calls.

Within moments, we arrived at his church.

A few of his church and business leaders were in the conference room. He asked me to share the details about ***God's Storehouse Principle*** while he apologized that the finance officer was not able to attend the meeting due to setting up a new office in Hong Kong.

When I trusted we were going to lunch, finally, the pastor actually invited me into a side office where we met and prayed with his church staff and leadership. It was so powerful and such a blessing.

We ran out of time for any part of a lunch, so he gave me a bottle of chilled water as we left the church. The water was perfect for my return to the conference to speak since I do not eat just before I speak. Perfection of God's plan!

This did begin a process of never getting the 'free lunch', however, God has a keen sense of humor.

My new pastor friend, Pastor Mark Smallcomb, became a special advocate and colleague while I was extended again and again in Australia. In fact, he invited me to preach in his church the next Sunday. He also invited me to speak at a business gathering of the leaders from the local churches. And, he included me with the 12 pastors working together in special meetings with Ed Silvoso[5] the next week. Mightily blessed!

Invitations by pastors to preach in the churches, and then, meet with their business leaders and speak with business teams within local corporations, and then, invitations by business executives to speak in their churches and this process continued for seven weeks!

On Sunday, Pastor Mark Smallcomb wanted me to share the ***God's Storehouse Principle*** facts I shared with the business and church leaders during our initial meetings.

When we gathered to pray before the service, he told me we needed to pray about a need for $10,000. I merely asked, **"...*what is the specific need?*"**

Again, Pastor Mark responded, **"*$10,000.*"**

So, I had to get serious because God was dealing with me immediately. God was being very clear with me, so I said exactly what God was saying in the same moment when God was saying it to me, *"God wants us to be very specific with the people ... if God handed you $10,000 right now ... what would the money be used for?"*

Finally, his reply was very specific, *"Welders."* So, I said, *"Let's join with the people in corporate prayer and ask God for your specific request, the welders you need."*

He looked surprised when he said, *"Our church is too young. The families in our church are young. Our offering is not much above $2000. so it's not going to be able to cover the costs. We need senior welders, to supervise a crew...and a crew..."*

God confirmed, again, that we need to be specific in our request, so I told Pastor Mark: *"We have to believe God seeds what is needed, He will provide, and we stand in faith in the process by asking the people and trusting the resources are available."*

While he was introducing me, he was almost apologizing for my belief that the specific prayer would result in the need being fulfilled without the funds being secured, but he was going to let me ask with eyes closed and heads bowed.

God was good! God provided more than enough welders, supervisors and hours to get the job done within the next week! This answer was only part of God's blessing. God also provided more than enough in the offering, and this Sunday together became the last Sunday the church was held in their leased location.

God provided everything required when we stood firm in faith and prayed for the specific needs, for the church to be in their new location the next Sunday.

The story was picked up by an international CBS TV affiliate for their version of the American CBS 60 Minutes program in Australia. So, what God did within a few moments that Sunday morning was shared across the nation within a few days.

My time in Australia was extended for seven weeks. Each week, God extended the time another seven days within 24 hours of confirming my new flight schedule with the local travel agency to confirm my flight home.

Encouraged, **Pastor Dewberry** left his laptop computer with me, so I could share the continued blessings with him and be in communication with prayer partners. We stayed in touch daily within emails, after he left at the end of his scheduled week, since he wanted to hear the 'new' news as he was amazed to observe all God was doing because I agreed to be available! I had no idea this would be how God would encourage Pastor Dewberry. This was a first experience of a pastor being encouraged to step into a higher level of faith by merely observing what God does through me.

It was an added blessing to be in the midst as Pastor Dewberry preached. He knows the demonic by name and calls them out, freeing the people and exactly as scripture confirms it causes their countenance to change! Many were delivered, set free and healed during the meetings.

Since I had to change the flight seven days in advance each time, it became a standing joke with my hostess. She laughed as each new invitation arrived which would require me to extend for seven days, again, because I was saying, ***"I would be glad to accept your invitation, however, I am scheduled to go home…"*** even though each time I booked the flight home in seven days, God extended my stay another seven days!

Pastor Mark included me within the group of twelve pastors meeting with Ed Silvoso and his ministry team, even though the team of pastors prepared for many weeks to be ready for the community outreach based upon the harvest plans shared by Ed Silvoso.

I was greeted by a young boy the night of the event. He handed me a piece of beige construction paper with a mouse holding on tight and peeking over the back of an elephant.[6]

The boy's parents were shocked. He only had a small backpack with him. They had no idea how he was able to bring a picture to me without folding it. They asked him about the picture and he responded, ***"God told me it was important for me to draw this and bring it with me. God said he would show me who to give it to."***

The picture meant a lot to me. Remember the mouse to the elephant analogy (key details are shared on page 22)? God does speak to the children! In that moment, I was experiencing God's confirmation of the people hearing the truth. I pray that we as the body of Christ would be ready to move forward.

Plans to be at a church in America for Passover changed to being in a church in downtown, Newcastle, Australia, and I went to the travel agent before the weekend, to ensure I would have a flight home for Easter! I was able to get the last seat on a flight. But, again, God had other plans.

Pastor Mark "*...the staff and business leaders heard the message of Personal & Professional Life Management this week, so we are blessed you agreed to preach the word to our church this morning.*"

Prayer Team "*We know now how we will we be able to continue this mighty work, when you are not in our midst...*"

Ephesians 1: 3-6. *Blessed be the God and Father of our Lord Jesus Christ, who has blessed us with every spiritual blessing in the heavenly places in Christ, [4] just as He chose us in Him before the foundation of the world, that we should be holy and without blame before Him in love, [5] having predestined us to adoption as sons by Jesus Christ to Himself, according to the good pleasure of His will, [6] to the praise of the glory of His grace, by which He made us accepted in the Beloved.*

Romans 8:16-17. *The Spirit Himself bears witness with our spirit that we are children of God, [17] and if children, then heirs—heirs of God and joint heirs with Christ, if indeed we suffer with Him, that we may also be glorified together.*

Chapter 14 Four Square, Aboriginal Cultural Center

Pastor Rex Morgan and Sheila Holm
Four Square Church, Aboriginal Cultural Center

While I was at the local hospital due to my host needing a series of tests, God prompted me to go for coffee in the coffee shop. I had no idea why, as I did not want coffee.

However, 'coffee shop' is exactly what they called the hospital cafe, so when I found out the name was specific I immediately walked to the location.

When I entered, a man was standing near the entrance. God said I was supposed to pray for him. So, I asked the man wearing a set of official hospital badges if it would be alright if I prayed for him.

The man was thrilled about the idea. He beamed from ear to ear. So, I took his hands in mine and looked into his eyes. As I began, the Holy Spirit quickly took over, anointed him with power and I was holding the back of his neck and helping him to land carefully on the floor.

Prayers continued, while it was not for the man. The prayers were for a child. The man smiled and said he had just prayed with a family for their child, while he remained flat on the floor. God asked me to continue praying in tongues for the man, so I did.

People entered & stepped right over the man, lying across the doorway.

The man smiled and raised his head a bit and said, **"You will speak to the women."** I kept praying and he went down in the power of the Holy Spirit once again.

Then, he raised his head slightly and said, *"You are to speak and pray with the men & the women"* and he went back down under the power of the Holy Spirit once again.

Then, he went into the gift of laughter and after a few minutes he raised his head slightly and said, *"OK God, she will preach in our church on Sunday."* I wanted to correct the man, as he was talking about Easter Sunday but, God was focused and said, *"Keep praying."*

A couple of minutes later, my hostess arrived. She helped me lift the man enough to get a chair under him. Before he could tell her about his plans for Sunday, I said, *"I will not be in Australia on Sunday ... you see, it is Easter ... I'm always with my family on Easter."*

While I was giving my excuses, I was being ignored.

I did not realize my hostess knew the man, a pastor, and they were talking and laughing about God confirming I would be preaching in his church on Sunday. They were making plans about the time I needed to arrive at the church, etc., and, I realized I could not have added one word even if they would have let me.

Then, my hostess said, *"Pastor Rex Morgan, you were just introduced to Sheila Holm."* Pastor said, **"Nice** to *meet you, Sheila Holm."*

And, there I was, on Easter Sunday, preaching in an Aboriginal Cultural Center at the Four Square Church for the region. God has such a special sense of humor – God gave me the basic scriptures in Ephesians about Family being where God places our feet ... and God blessed the congregation by all in the room being empowered by the Holy Spirit due to the anointing ... even the usher, the founder of the first RHEMA radio station in Australia. The family decided to retire in the community and give back to the people who welcomed them and gave so much to them when they arrived.

A line of women stood before me. I started praying with the youngest one, first. Each one went down, and as I reached the end of the line, I was just beginning the prayer as the woman went down and I was still with her, praying with her, as I felt a tug on my skirt. The youngest girl said she had to ask me a question.

"Sure, what do you want to know?" I asked, as I noticed she was beaming!

"God told me he sent you to me!" She was so excited, as she asked, *"So, how did God send you to me?"* Ah, the same question as the young men in Dallas.

Well, I went into Sheila logic. I told her I'm from San Diego and I shared details from a flight itinerary mode, letting her know about airlines, and she said, *"God did not say that."*

So, I told her names of the towns where I caught the flights, and yet, again, she said, *"God did not say that."*

So, I said I came from the United States, but, again, she said, **"God** *did not say that."*

So, I said, *"We need to pray and ask God, specifically."* But, she was too excited to stop and be quiet to pray with me, so she said, *"God told me he sent you to me."*

In that moment God told me to tell her, **"I'm** *from America…"* and she jumped for joy as she said, *"That's it. God said he sent you from America to Australia for me. So, I just* *want to know, when God sends you to me what type of plane does God use?"*

Speechless! She rendered me speechless. I was trying to answer her in the natural. She was still in the supernatural with the Holy Spirit and she knew God had arranged for my ticket to be with her. God orchestrates beyond our natural comprehension!

In the middle of the service, the sky had opened and the rain poured down! Three young men on motor bikes came in out of the rain. They noticed the food brought by the people attending the church service, so they decided to come in and get out of the rain. The only open seats were three in the middle of the second row, directly in front of me. They appeared to be very interested in what I was saying.

After the service, when the people started to get up off the floor, the three young men joined the prayer line. One of the three asked me, **"What does that man want from me?"** So, I asked him, "Which man?" He said, "That one," as he pointed to the name *Jesus* Christ on my scarf and said, **"He's been talking to me. I can hear Him, but I can't see Him."**

As I was saying, **"Jesus is calling you to Him."** The young man said, **"Yes, he wants me ... I don't know what he wants from me."** So, I said, **"It's simple. He wants you."**

As I held the back of his neck and started to pray, he went down under the power of the Holy Spirit. At the same time, Pastor

Rex Morgan had a word of knowledge that someone in the room had a pain in their ankle and they should come forward.

The young man got up off the floor and said, *"That's me. My ankle has been hurting since you prayed for me."*

So, I told him, *"God knows you have experienced a severe hurt, a deep pain, and you are holding on to it but, if you release it now the pain will go away and Jesus will replace your pain with his peace."*

The young man was immediately sobbing as he said, *"My fiance was shot. She died in my arms. I left Sydney on a walk about. I just arrived in this area and went riding with these men this morning ..."*

The three young men came to Christ in that moment. They requested Holy Spirit 'in-filling.' Pastor Rex had another word of knowledge that one of them would be a guitar player in the band – the same young man said he always wanted to play the guitar, but, he did not know music and he never had an opportunity to hold a guitar. One of the praise team members handed him a guitar. He started to play, right then and there, and it was as if he had played the guitar his entire life. The praise team band joined with him. The music was great. God is so good!

The seven weeks were filled with glorious details, as was this day already, but, to grasp what God was saying to this young girl in this moment, God had orchestrated all of these details, to send me from America to Australia for this young girl ... wow. And, even in hind sight saying it backwards, wow!

And, that's not all. The line of women were from the same family! The great, great grandmother had prayed her family into the church, and they agreed to come on this Sunday and share the meal served because it was Easter Sunday!

The women before me were the generations of one family.

The prayers over the years had resulted in their gathering together and being blessed and brought to the feet of Jesus on this Easter Sunday!

What did God need me to do? Pray for a man wearing a hospital badge. Then, all I had to do was extend my trip one more time!

Covenant Agreement

In the afternoon, God added a meeting. A business owner, a pastor, and their wives, met with me to pray about their agreement. Within seconds, God revealed the two couples proceeded without an agreement.

A covenant agreement was needed and it was not outlined prior to the meeting. Not an easy meeting, but we did outline an agreement!

The pastor's wife was new to me. It was a tough discussion for her and it was held in her home. I kept praying with God to confirm she was being blessed.

In those moments, she left the room and returned with a book she handed to me as a gift.

Have you heard of the missionary Rees Howells[7]?

He repeatedly describes how God provides as each need was identified and declared during his hours, days in fasting and prayer. The Holy Spirit would tell him who to talk to and the action steps to take. God even told him to go to his mail box at one point to receive what God provided to cover the need so Rees could take on the next assignment.

His story is very similar to the 'Faith Walk' of Pastor Harald Bredesen and now, the giver of the gift is saying the faith walk Rees Howells was on is exactly like the faith walk God is directing for me and I pray he will direct the same faith walk for you, also.

The pastor's wife saw the similarity between what God was doing with me and what God had done with Rees. I thank God for the special confirmation the details blessed her.

Matthew 10:9 *"Do not take gold or silver or copper in your belts (purse); take no bag for the journey, or extra tunic…for the worker is worth his keep."*

Without an extra coin or tunic…God provided three Australian suits and many offerings. Blessings paid the bills during this time and I was shocked, because I had $600 left over. At least, I thought it was going to be 'extra' as I was packing to fly home within 24 hours.

Can God Use One Person To Change A Nation?

God had a new plan unfolding, while I trusted I was going home within 24 hours.

During my stay, a business man provided a magazine article about the Kingdom of Tonga. The headline was a quote by the Minister Tasi, the Minister of Finance in Tonga, *"We Must Change or We Will Die."*

Prayers brought the pastor in the region together with my host family. They shared calls, and the pastor knew I was supposed to come.

The flight, however, required $1200. Since they were not able to provide the ticket, I trusted I would not be able to go. They immediately put a prayer team together. They fasted and prayed, while I was continually extended, week, after week, after week, in Australia!

The prayer partners of my host family met to pray with us. A phone call required the attention of my hostess, so a woman asked if I was going to pray about Tonga.

My hostess and I laughed, while my hostess was still on her call. I looked at her and asked her if she shared the Tonga details… she said, *"NO!"*

The woman felt we should pray, as I was supposed to go to Tonga. In that moment, I stopped laughing. I told the woman the funds were not available to fly to Tonga. She was still praying. Then, she asked if I made a deal with God. I told her that I only had half of the money for the ticket and then, I remembered, so I told her I did tell God, *"...if God arranged for the rest of the ticket, I would be willing to go."*

She laughed and said, *"Sounds like a deal to me!"*

My hostess was able to join hands with us. As soon as she said, *"Let's pray,"* the phone rang. My hostess tried to tell the caller we were in the middle of prayer, but, the man said his call was urgent. The Lord prompted the caller to call in that moment and offer $600. He wanted the details shared during the initial meeting with Pastor Smallcomb's church leadership during my first day in Newcastle, Australia!

Within the hour, I was on a flight to Sydney and on to Fiji to meet with the pastor I prayed for in America which led to the trip to Australia. This was not in the plan, prior to the flight to Tonga! God knew, but I was 'completely unaware' of this part of the plan!

God's Orchestration to Complete the Assignment in Australia

When I arrived at the local airport in Newcastle for the commuter flight to Sydney, a man asked if I was the American speaking in the area. When I merely nodded, as I was finalizing my ticket details, he said, *"I know the pilot. I take this flight all of the time. I'll move our seats so we can talk during the flight, if that's OK with you."*

"Of course," I said, as the flight attendant made the adjustments so we would be assigned adjoining seats. God knew –

the man was the finance officer of Pastor Mark Smallcomb's church, the first church I met with. The man Pastor Mark had confirmed as his finance officer who was in Hong Kong. Since he missed the initial meeting and the Sunday service when I preached, the Lord arranged for us to be on the same flight. He was flying to Sydney, to catch a flight to London. We talked. He received helpful information for his meetings, regarding his acquisition of a new division. God was so good to us!

The man arranged for the taxi to the international terminal and he handed me $50. I was thrilled, but, I was not sure why. Then, he quickly stated, *"God said it's for your next taxi."* It was a quick trip to my next taxi! As I entered the terminal, I was immediately advised that I was going to be charged an over limit fee. You guessed it. $50 exactly!

Without an extra coin, I am ready for the next assignment. God's orchestration is amazing! And, God arranged a last minute surprise for me. The next destination was not Tonga, it was a meeting with the pastor in Fiji.

Bottom line: I arrived without cash, without an extra coin. I was richly blessed. I was hosted by special prayer partners who adopted me into their family. I was given tunics, but, per God's perfect orchestration here I am, again, without cash, aka an extra coin!

Aimee Semple McPherson, founder of the global Four Square Church which had spread to 67 countries during her lifetime: *"Give your heart to God. Come and help me. With salvation, baptism of the Holy Spirit and divine healing ... Are you born again? Does anyone know that you're saved? Let the world know that you're on the Lord's side. If you're a soldier of the King and a soldier of the cross, then fight the good fight of faith. Grow up to be men and women, filled with the spirit and glorifying God ... be willing to live according to* **Acts 2:4. And they were all filled with the Holy Spirit and began to speak with other tongues, as the Spirit gave them utterance.** *... and lay down their lives for the sake of the Gospel."*

Sheila Holm *"Because the Lord knows I always spend Easter with family, God has confirmed we are family by placing my feet in the midst of this assembly and giving me a word to share with you for we are joint heirs with Christ."*

Chapter 15 God's Orchestration: Fiji & Tonga

Fiji

Only God knew I would be flying to Tonga with a required 'over night stay' in Fiji. The Fiji pastor met me at the airport with his family. What a blessing.

It was the middle of the night. The airport was at the opposite side of the island from his home.

We spent the entire night driving north, praying and sharing. Then, we met and prayed in his home the rest of the night, as the sun was coming up and throughout the next day until the very moment when I had to return to the airport to go on to Tonga.

God was so good. The prayers deeply touched the senior pastor and each member of his family.

They were so kind. They worried about the fact there was 'no sleep' for me, but there is only one flight into Tonga each week and one flight out. So, we had to rush to squeeze in all that God wanted us to do within the few hours we had available!

They wanted me to rest, to sleep, because they are used to a set sleeping schedule. With God, however, the human sleeping schedule is easily replaced with a few moments being blessed by the Holy Spirit. God energizes deeper, faster and more efficiently than a nap or a night of rest!

The schedule worked out perfectly.

We do serve an awesome God!

Kingdom of Tonga

When God confirmed the flight was going to be arranged to Tonga, my host called the pastor in Tonga, Pastor Isileli Taukolo. He was in tears.

God had just released their prayer team from fasting and prayer, with the confirmation I was coming. Pastor Isileli just entered his door and crossed the threshold, as the phone rang.

Trusted all was 'in order' until I heard the news while I was waiting in the Fiji airport for my flight to Tonga, the Prince and brother of the King has passed away. The entire nation was in mourning and they would be in mourning for the entire week, until the funeral of the Prince.

Pastor Isileli met me at the airport in the capital of Tonga, Nuku'AlofaNu. When I asked about the meetings, the purpose for my visit, he responded, *"Not to worry."*

I did not realize in this moment what I would come to know as the very mantra of pastor Isileli. To every question or concern his automatic and immediate response was the same as the famous Crocodile Dundee quote, *"Not to worry."*

We made one stop to pick up bottled water and a large can of bug spray.

Little did I realize how critical both items would be in that moment. However, their significance was made perfectly clear to me as soon as I arrived at the home of my host family!

Within seconds, Pastor Isileli confirmed the meetings may not take place as God had confirmed, due to the funeral plans.

My heart sank, for I was sure I was supposed to be in Tonga this week, and the only flight out of Tonga was in a week, next Tuesday after the weekend funeral!

The pastor reminded my hostess the water needed to be boiled, as did the food they would prepare for me. Then, I was shown to my room, which was a guest house with a pot of boiling water waiting for me in case I wanted to wash my hair or take a quick shower with a garden hose to provide the cool water. This was required since their home did not have hot running water.

One thing was sure. It was going to be a very special week in my life!

Little did I realize the many years growing up on the farm were actually years of being trained for such a time as this!

Before I closed my eyes, there was something I needed to do prior to entering into the mosquito netting which surrounded the bed. I forgot to carry the can of bug spray to bed with me to keep next to my pillow.

It became an important can which I needed to carry with me everywhere. I quickly grew a close affinity to the large spray can after I was very busy using it throughout the night. Each time I sprayed, I asked God for another confirmation of His plans for this week, because I was not certain why I was in Tonga if I was not going to able to meet with and bless the people.

The next morning I was greeted by Sela, my interpreter. She was assigned to help me for the week. She was carrying a large tray of fruit and toast as she entered the guest house.

The papayas in Tonga are huge, very orange and they are very good! By the end of the week, I was trying to arrange an export business to ship the papayas from Tonga to America instead of shipping them to Hawaii and then, Hawaii shipping smaller papayas to America. This venture was still 'a conversation' when I left Tonga, and, as of today, the opportunity is still 'a deal, in process.'

Sela arranged for meetings with departments of the Government. Since they are a Christian nation we were able to pray within the government buildings. It was fabulous!

God also provided a special introduction to the Minister of Finance, Minister Tasi, the man featured in the business articles shared by business leaders while I was in Australia. Only God knew that my interpreter, Sela, who took me on a tour of the island and interpreted the messages God shared through me during the prayer sessions in the government and business offices, and during the church services, actually works in the Ministry of Finance for Minister Tasi. The Holy Spirit prompted her to request the introduction by Pastor Isileli or she was going to introduce me to Minister Tasi on Monday morning.

My prayers were diligent, as the time I had left was Monday and part of Tuesday. Early Monday morning, Pastor Isileli called to confirm I would be meeting with Minister Tasi in the afternoon.

Tears, as I continued to pray about the meeting. Pieces of papaya were the only food I took in during the day, while I continued to pray and trust God would give me the right words to share during the meeting, to bless Minister Tasi and the people within the Treasury and Ministry of Finance.

Pastor Isileli picked me up. When we arrived at the government building, Sela greeted us and offered to be my interpreter. The Minister stood and shook my hand. He is quite tall. He speaks perfect English. He told Sela he would like her to make some copies of documents for me.

Pastor Isileli stayed near the doorway, as Minister Tasi sat across from me and began the introduction process. He let me know of his many degrees and bible training.

Tears filled my eyes as I continued to pray while I heard his many accomplishments, top global university degrees and he's also a bible scholar.

Thanking God for taking over when it was time for me to respond. I could only say, **"I've obtained a few degrees, I'm not a bible scholar, but, I trust God has sent me as His servant to serve you …"** and, when I took a breath I noticed a strange tapping sound.

I looked at the pastor; he was in tears. Then, I looked at Minister Tasi and he was in tears. Their tears were falling on their wraps, a wrap which all Tongans wear, and that was making the sound I heard.

Minister Tasi stood up and told me, **"Tomorrow, I will close the offices and our leaders will meet with you. We will fill the room …"** God took over. It was as though I was swept up in the glory of God in that moment. I was no longer hearing any words or activities of the people around me.

I saw the pastor making schedule arrangements with the staff. I noticed my hand was outstretched and I was shaking hands with the Minister, his staff, and Sela, before departing. I was still not hearing any words from people as I walked to the pastor's car.

The introduction was made by the Holy Spirit. I merely 'showed up'.

This experience was so surreal. To this day, I'm still not able to remember any other details about that meeting. However, God has extended his sense of humor about introductions, because I've been introduced to speak and when a speaker does not appear, I am asked to speak merely because I 'showed up' for the meeting. This has happened on several occasions since my special introduction to Minister Tasi, the Minister of Finance for The Kingdom of Tonga.

Newspaper Headline: Government Office Closed

The Honorable Minister of Finance, Tasi, canceled the schedule for the top 30 senior staff of the government the next day. A seminar was provided in the morning and individual coaching for the government leaders was provided in the afternoon, with a specific scripture being shared from the Lord for each man participating. The words were given per the prompting of the Holy Spirit because my bible was already packed in my luggage. God was good to me by giving me the words! It was a full day!

After Minister Tasi introduced the program, the seminar was conducted without one smile or reaction from one of the participants in the room. I was concerned because I felt they were not blessed. When I finished, I asked the Minister, but, he merely responded by stating the lunch would be served. Silence continued, as plates and lace cloths were placed before each of us, stacked with warm sandwiches.

Then, Minister Tasi asked the Minister of Land Revenue to stand and share a word of blessing with me to confirm how he was blessed. The man stood. He was so deeply touched it was difficult for him to speak, but he began listing the many things that deeply touched him. It was so difficult for him to continue speaking about how deeply I had blessed him through the words I shared. The tears were so abundant. His voice so shaken, the Minister thanked him as he asked the next Minister to stand.

Minister Tasi asked the Minister of Internal Revenue to share how the words had blessed him. He was even more emotional about how my words had blessed him, and I was so shocked and touched, and in awe of what God had done, while I was clearly unaware that I was unable to even munch on my lunch for how deeply God had blessed each one, through me merely because I agreed to 'show up.'

It was such a blessing to be able to include the scriptures throughout the seminar, as it is rare in the world to be able to share God's words, especially in a government building in America as the scriptures relate directly to the business principles we are to operate within on a daily basis. Oh, how God blessed me!

Oh yes, the blessings! God provided two tunics and multiple blessings. Minister Tasi wrote a beautiful letter of acknowledgment and inserted a significant cash payment for the seminar within the envelope. Yes. I was blessed!

God's plan was evident again. I would be taking the next assignment without cash in hand, aka an extra coin.

I was not aware of the fact Tongan currency does not transfer into other currency outside of Tonga. When I returned home, I returned the payment to Minister Tasi to bless the local businesses, since I was reminded by God of the plans for my journey, as Jesus told the apostles to travel: **Matthew 10:9** *"Do not take gold or silver or copper in your belts (purse); take no bag for the journey, or extra tunic...for the worker is worth his keep."*

There was an added blessing! Since I had a night time lay-over, again, Minister Tasi sent a government official on the flight from Tonga to Fiji and he instructed the Minister to pay my hotel bill and make all arrangements in Fiji to assure me that I had no other costs to cover in my travel back to Australia. The Minister paid the over limit baggage fee, and they arranged for first class travel! My luggage was checked through to America, so I did not have another fee to worry about.

While I was transitioning at the Sydney airport for my return flight to America, Jocelyn, the conference coordinator for the initial conference during my first days in Australia met me for lunch. It was fabulous to have a moment to share the testimonies of the Tongan journey and to hear how the details had blessed the team, especially since they were prompted by God to invest the balance of my flight ticket to Tonga.

Jocelyn wanted to know if I thought the investment of all of the funds for a flight ticket was worth it. The answer was easy, **"God** *sent me to meet the pastor in Fiji and I had no other way to meet with him. God touched and changed lives and future plans in Tonga and no amount of money could do what God did to impact and change a nation. I was richly and mightily blessed."* God's provision was more than coins and tunics on this amazing journey!

Pastor Isileli Taukolo *"Our board and business leaders were fasting and praying and God confirmed He was sending someone to us. We are deeply touched by the message God sent to us, through you."*

Minister of Finance, Tasi *"Our meeting was an answer to my prayers, and I thank you for providing the seminar for our senior staff members, and meeting with them individually for prayer and coaching."*

Government Office *"Thank you for speaking today and for staying and praying with us…"*

Chapter 16 New Assignment Before I Was Unpacked

While I was unpacking, I heard a knock at the door.

A 'fellow Lutheran' arrived to deliver a special card and God told her a cash amount to place in the card. I was shocked. When I asked her about God's message, she said it was an amount that would be required for my next journey.

Then, she handed me a journal, as she told me she was also prompted to pick up a journal at the Christian bookstore. She trusted I should journal what God is doing in my life. So, I told her about the lap top loaned to me by Pastor Dewberry and she offered to let me use her home phone line to check email messages. That's right, it was when we were on 'dial up internet' vs high speed internet!

We shared a late lunch before I checked the email messages.

To my surprise, I had an invitation to be in London the next day ... so, my friend let me call the airlines and I had more than enough frequent flyer miles to go. They wanted a fee to exchange the points at the last minute. So, since that was not feasible, as I could not put a fee on a card and the airlines required days to process the fee before I could obtain the ticket, I had to share a bit of my testimony so the employee would understand I had to leave at oh dark thirty the next morning. Within a couple of minutes, the woman said, *"I'm off tomorrow morning ... I'll meet you at the airport ticket counter ... I'll take care of everything ... then, we'll go into the airline club when you arrive so I can hear more details about what God is doing..."*

Well, I knew (in my limited human mind) that was not possible, so I started to explain I am not authorized to go into the Airline club, when she said, *"It will be arranged for you ... just give them your flight confirmation number and I will be waiting inside ..."* She processed my ticket without a fee and provided the confirmation number, which concluded the call. I was in shock, and now, in a major hurry to pack!

My friend was laughing, since this information confirmed she had clearly heard God's message while she was at the Christian book store.

It was amazing. She was not aware of the fact I had returned from my travels, yet, but God prompted her to personally deliver the card.

She made sure that I was reminded to follow God's instructions: 1. take the journal, 2. begin journaling all God is doing in these days, 3. take the cash for the next journey, and 4. insert the card as a bookmark for the journal, since she knew God selected the card and she wanted the encouraging words to be with me as I traveled to London. She gave me her email address to keep her updated, also.

She was so considerate and calm, while I was not. OK, I'll admit it. I was in a bit of a panic! I had to re-pack from being down under in 100 degree heat and 100% humidity, nearly every day, to being in London with 40-50 degree temperatures during the day, with cool breezes … I needed to focus and make a plan. Yikes!

Heathrow Airport, London

When I arrived, nobody greeted me. So, I called my host. She was not returning 'from holiday' until the next morning. She trusted I would take a day to pack and then a day to fly, and to my surprise, our days are one day off between California and London, due to the fact London is ahead of us by an eight hour time change. Yikes!

Still 'with lap top' since the time was not available to return it to Pastor Dewberry, and I was still traveling, I quickly searched for a business office to check messages.

The Information Desk directed me through a series of tunnels, with my overflowing baggage cart, to a terminal location for the business office. As in the movie ***Star Wars***, the location was far, far away.

To my surprise, the sign on the door confirmed the business office is actually closed that day, each week. Heartsick and many tunnels away from the Information Desk, my only option was to reverse the significant luggage cart and return the way I came. So, I pushed the luggage cart back through the various tunnels to the Information Desk in the terminal building where I landed.

There had been a change of shift. New staff recommended I take the shuttle to a local hotel, since they have a business office. OK.

But, where was the shuttle location? I'll tell you if you promise not to laugh. The shuttle picks up directly in front of the building where they house the business office, so off I ventured, once again, to push the luggage cart, again, through what had become a lengthy yet familiar tunnel path to me by now, turning sharp turns on so-so luggage cart wheels to continue through tunnel to tunnel to tunnel.

The challenge to load the luggage into the shuttle had to be comical for anyone with a view of the shuttle entrance door! The driver is evidently not an employee known as a luggage loader. Evidently the luggage loader employee had the day off. Did I mention that I had a winter coat, hat, gloves, and they did not fit into the luggage? They were precariously positioned on the top of the luggage cart and now the carry-on luggage and bag, plus winter coat, hat and gloves were all in my lap. I want to be sure the visual is accurate and complete.

Finally, my luggage was on the shelves of the shuttle and we were off!

We arrived at the Radisson near the airport. The staff was very accommodating, while I cautioned them I was not checking in, I was only at the hotel to check emails and not to spend the night. They set my luggage to the side as I searched for the business office to check emails.

The staff was busy closing the business office for the day. However, they allowed me to plug in the lap top while positioning it on top of a chair in the hallway to check messages. To my surprise, there were no messages from pastors or business leaders regarding invitations yet, so I returned to the front desk.

As I approached the desk, I noticed everyone was wearing evening attire, except me. I must have had a look of 'left over from a long, long flight' since the men in the group took one look, backed up and away from the counter as they said, *"Help her."*

Trying to smile as I began the story about my host not returning 'from holiday' until tomorrow when a man walked up to the counter and said, *"Give her the bridal party rate ..."* and just that quick, I had a room – the deal was done!

Good news! I felt rich as I heard the room rate, since I could quickly calculate the balance and it left a good amount of cash to purchase dinner and breakfast ... until I heard the clerk state, **"The room rate is in British pounds, not American dollars."**

My heart sank. I took a deep breath as I prepared to ask her if I had enough, when she quickly saved me from embarrassment by saying, **"You have to pay an exchange rate fee, so the balance to you is a little more than two pounds."**

As though she heard my inner voice asking what could I find to eat for about two pounds, she said, **"McDonald's is next door to the hotel, just turn left when you exit the front and you will see it..."**

That night, I dined as a 'Kingdom Kid' since a kid's meal at the local McDonald's was the only order that was in my price range!

There was some laughter amongst the tears during prayers that night, since God had tapped the shoulder of a friend in San Diego to buy the card, insert the amount of cash required upon my arrival in London to have a great place to rest, and to purchase a journal for me to begin to write all of the glorious orchestration details God was arranging on my behalf, before I left home. And then, with a member of the bridal party in London being positioned by God to provide a reduced rate, to ensure God's provision was 'enough' for the journey, as I continued on my 'Faith Walk!' I was grateful!

Oh, and God arranged breakfast at no cost! My host arranged to pick me up in the morning and brought some tea and fresh croissants. It was fabulous!

We met through a mutual friend over the phone only, while she was living in Australia a couple of years before. She was deeply touched to hear my stories of Australia, especially since God had arranged for me to be in the New South Wales region, which is where she had lived prior to moving to London the prior year.

We shared glorious details about these days over the next couple of days.

Then, she told me that she had lost hope in the Lord's provision, so she showed me Jaeger hangers in her closet, stating she would have new suits on those hangers within weeks. This status brought tears to my eyes. She had lost faith in who God is and how God operates. My testimony was not encouraging her to regain her faith …

My words were falling on deaf ears. I would not have believed it, if I had not seen it for myself. Diligent prayers to seek God's plan for this day…to know what God would have me do.

God confirmed I was to check my emails. An invitation had just arrived to journey to a London Doctor's country home and rest over the weekend, and then, journey by train to downtown London for meetings with a prayer team on Tuesday.

Bishop John Francis presented his CD, _Finally_, a blessing to me again & again & again, plus he shared a personal acknowledgment: *"God is doing a mighty work through you ... God orchestrated our introduction while you were introducing other pastors to me ... we need to spend more time together about what God is revealing ... "*

Chapter 17 God Orchestrates A New Plan

After the prayer team meeting, I was granted a place to stay with a member of the team. As soon as we arrived at her home, my hostess said she had gone to her country home over the weekend since God had prompted her to bring back a suit that she had stored in the closet. It was a suit she had always admired, but it was not her size. God was prompting her to give it to me, since I will be in a power meeting, soon, and I will need that suit.

To my utter amazement she returned to the living room with a brand new Jaeger suit still hanging on the Jaeger hangers with the price tag evident. We laughed about the tag, while it did not concern her at all, as she stood in awe when we immediately realized the suit jacket fit me like a glove!

Then, she said, ***"OK, God"*** as she left the living room again. She returned with another new suit, designed by a French designer, again with the price tags still attached. And part of the humor about this story I have to share in this part of the book, ahead of schedule since you will enjoy this little tidbit: both of the suits made the trip home to California in perfect condition; I have the suits, but, not the hangers! The Jaeger hangers were very sturdy and substantial, but both hangers were broken!

Bottom line: I have no Jaeger hangers to hang in my closet, but, God provided the suit which would have cost a good amount, if I would have been 'working in the world' every hour I was in London in order to have enough cash to purchase the suit myself! I am grateful to be a servant of the most-high God!

God's Travel Plans Included Family Connections

My Dad's family is from Norway, and I had not been to Norway. To my surprise, my hostess had not been to Norway, either, and she received confirmation from the Lord of a journey we were to take to Norway and to Sweden, by way of Copenhagen.

God confirmed the brief stay in Copenhagen was only due to a meeting at a restaurant in the airport, so we only arranged for hotel stays in Oslo, Norway and Malmo, Sweden.

Since I had exactly the right number of frequent flyer miles to fly to Norway, and while I am using the miles, the airlines provide coupons for 'free hotel stays' every other night at a Radisson. It was time to pray over the details.

My hostess immediately agreed to share the costs by paying the alternate night hotel stays, and that finalized the travel arrangements. We were off on a journey God was orchestrating.

Time would be tight in Norway, because God confirmed we had a special appointment in a Copenhagen airport restaurant, on the way to Malmo, Sweden.

God's plans for the timing and details were so specific. When I started to doubt my ability to navigate through Norway, I asked God, ***"How can I possibly find my family in such a short period of time?"*** But, God confirmed he would make the arrangements, and I trusted!

Norway

We landed in Oslo, Norway, and quickly found the best option to get to the Trondheim area: the night train to Stjordal. It was great to see the name of the town where my Grandfather was raised. Personally, I looked at it many times, daily, since it is printed in gold on the special gift from my parents, after they visited with our relatives, years before. And, I knew it would be the right area, as my Grandfather shared stories when I was young, about being raised near the Trondheim fjord.

Travel on the night train was fabulous. Each stop was exciting, even though it went on and on, all night long! The lights appeared each time we slowed down, because we went through the mountain areas, and the towns were lit up like Christmas when we arrived! I simply had to get up and look out the window each time!

Very little sleep, but, I was not tired, I was OK with a quick decision to go straight to the local hotel (visible from the train station) to drop off our luggage and go directly to the church, as I trusted I would be able to find my relatives there. I thought we were early and would have time for breakfast. However, it was confirmation Sunday at the Stjordal Vaernes Kirke, and the families were in their native family/regional attire, as they entered the church.

Their outfits were absolutely beautiful. Their dress made our Sunday dress stand out and immediately identify us as the 'foreigners' in their church! Instead of ushering us to the back, as we entered, they asked if we had relatives in the church, so I told them 'Holm' and we were whisked up the aisle, and ushered to the front row.

The church is majestic in wood and a carved altar, and every section of the church is in perfect condition. It was designed and carved in wood, and in that region and with their winters it should show it's age, but, you would think they enjoyed perfect weather the year round, since the church is impeccably maintained, inside and out. You would never know the building was over 900 years old.

The pastor was so busy with the families after the confirmation service, and yet, I needed his help since I was diligently searching but, had no idea how I would be able to recognize my relatives in the crowd. To my surprise, no relatives were in the service, as the families not involved in the confirmation do not attend. Instead, they leave room for all of the relatives of the confirmation class on this special Sunday. And, little did I realize, that at any time in my lifetime would I have difficulty identifying which Holm might be a Holm I would be related to!

We prayed together with the pastor and staff, then, it was time for plan B. We returned to the hotel so I could try to find someone who would know details about my family.

The manager said she would help. She handed me the phone book!

So, I prayed. Then, I opened to the Holm name and found at least 50 options, I diligently prayed! God directed me to a long, hyphenated name and I prayed as I dialed the number. In the same moment the phone was ringing, their granddaughter entered the house and picked up the phone. A gift from God, because she understood English!

Quickly, I started listing the names of aunts and uncles that had visited Stjordal over the years. Then, the names and details were being translated and shared in Norwegian with the residents of the house. Within moments, there were screams in the background, because the family thought I was one of my aunts, Aunt Ella! We quickly cleared up the confusion, so they would know I am the niece of Aunt Ella, and then, they screamed again to realize my parents visited with them a few years ago. The best news was, as we identified the various family members, it was clear that we were related!

They invited me to their home for afternoon coffee. There was a sea of food on the table when we arrived, along with a bottomless pot of coffee! Each time one piece of food was picked up, a replacement piece appeared. It was magical. They invited additional cousins to enjoy our lengthy "almost lost in translation" conversations and coffee. The cameras were flashing and there was a lot of laughter, as my comments were translated into Norwegian, especially the few lines for the guest book. It was amazing to be signing the pages that were signed by my relatives during their journey to Norway, and especially to see the handwriting of my mother, many years before!

Seemed so quick, and yet, God was providing everything within the short time frame available, since I had a 'date' to be in an airport restaurant in Copenhagen. It was not easy to break away from them, but, it was a glorious time together, and I had to depart for Oslo that night to take the early flight to Copenhagen the next morning.

Copenhagen

When we landed in Copenhagen, we were close to our flight gate for Malmo, which is always a nice surprise.

God was clear that an assignment awaited us in the airport restaurant, so I asked where the restaurant near our gate area is located. Each airport employee laughed, as they tried to think of any restaurant beyond the one, the main and only restaurant in the entire airport, which is located exactly at the opposite end of the airport!

OK. I started evaluating how hungry I was feeling. But, my London hostess and witness for these days just laughed and said, "We know which restaurant God was talking about, since it is the only one ... and, we may be hungry by the time we get way over there!" and, with that comment, she pointed at the map. We laughed and began our trek, heading across the entire length of the airport. God's keen sense of humor!

The manager appeared to be worried. The restaurant was full. We were not worried, because we knew we were 'on assignment.'

Immediately upon seating us in the very back corner, it was evident the woman next to us was alone and upset. When I asked her if she was alright, she said, *"Seven years of a journey to find my purpose, my spiritual path. I've been to Nepal, I've met with the gurus of many religions. Now, I'm on a flight home in a couple of minutes and I'm still lost, I'm going home empty."*

I asked her if it was alright to pray together, because God can fill her to overflowing in a couple of minutes. She tried to muster a smile through the tears, as she nodded her head.

God revealed that she had been with what the world refers to as spiritual masters around the globe, but she had not experienced what only God can offer to her, so I asked her, *"Would you like Jesus Christ to enter into your life, into your heart, and replace your emptiness, your pain with a peace that passes all understanding ... so you can go home fulfilled and ready to live your life?"* and she continued to nod, so, I continued, *"...then, in your own words, invite Christ into your life right now, to become your Savior ... your comforter ... and he will ..."* as the tears flowed, she made her choice and declared her request.

Then, I asked her if she would like the Holy Spirit to enter in and fill her and guide her each of her days, and she continued to nod through her tears, so, I took out my little vile of anointing oil, and I anointed her head and ears and eyes and throat (voice) and hands with anointing oil, and as I anointed her feet for her journey home and beyond, she went into the gift of laughter with the Holy Spirit.

Tears of joy covered her face. Praise God, her countenance had changed!

She was smiling as she hugged me, and then, she hugged my witness and checked her watch. *"Perfect timing. God operates in perfect timing..."* as she smiled, grabbed her bag, but then, she stopped for one more moment to look at me and hug me again before she rushed out of the restaurant to catch her flight home as a new woman in Christ.

We quickly ordered a sandwich to go, because we were out of time to stay and eat lunch due to the fact we were at the opposite end of the airport so we had a long trek back to our gate for our flight!

We rushed up to the gate to hear the announcement of a hydro jet boat to Malmo departing out of our same gate, at the exact same time. I found this to be a very strange announcement.

As we approached the gate, I noticed the passengers descending a flight of stairs. I quickly showed the flight attendant my ticket, and she said, *"Yes. You will be departing for the boat in a few moments."*

As fast as I could talk, I tried to explain, *"I do not 'do boats.' There has to be a mistake, a very big mistake with the reservation. My ticket has a plane symbol next to my flight number. See? It's a plane symbol and not a boat symbol. I'm in an airport to take a plane to Malmo."*

The attendant smiled, and she was very gracious and calm as she said, *"There are no flights to Malmo. The only way to get to Malmo is to take the boat..."*

So, I said things in my head to God! Of course it did not matter because I knew I was headed to Malmo, and I was out of time to make changes. My witness laughed, as she realized how serious I was about this status not being right so she tried to assure me by reminding me, *"I trust God knew about your fear, so he worked very hard to keep you very busy so you would not be sitting in this gate the entire time and worrying about the change in the mode of transportation to Malmo! Remember, you are the one that is always saying God has a keen sense of humor!"*

And, God does.

And, God confirmed we had to be in Malmo.

So, the facts were clear. And yet, I had to remind myself, God already knew I was going to be on a boat in a few minutes. God knew long before this journey started. So, to find out what God had 'in store' for me in Malmo, I had to trust He did not bring me to this place and lay out this plan, to have me experience a problem on a boat that was required to complete my trip to Malmo!

Sweden

First trip to Sweden and the scenery was breathtaking.

We arrived at the hotel late afternoon, so it was good to have a moment to rest and refresh before meeting for dinner. When we met, we did not have 'new' news to share about God's plans for these days, so we decided to continue praying and then, gather together in the morning for breakfast and compare notes.

God was quiet. Everything was quiet. God only confirmed it was a time of rest.

While resting in the room after dinner on the second night and praying with my hostess, witness, and new prayer partner, the phone rang.

Thinking it was the front desk, so it was a complete shock when I heard the voice of The Honorable Minister of Finance in Tonga, Minister Tasi! He shared emails a few times since the days in Tonga, but, his call was a complete surprise!

He was inviting me to extend my stay in Europe instead of returning to America immediately upon my return to London.

Sharing the truth with him about my frequent flyer ticket only being available for the exact day of my return to London (May 15 flying to London and departing London for America), otherwise the return ticket would not available again for several months (October 15), plus the fact that I could not be stuck in London for several months, so, I trusted they would want to re-schedule the London meetings.

But, he continued to stress the fact that this time frame was critical due to the schedule for the Global Economic Summit. So, I told him I would need to purchase another flight ticket if I was going to be extended in London. He said that would not be a problem since the blessing for their Embassy in London would be of more value than the cost of a flight ticket.

So, I agreed. Then, since I had to know, I asked, *"How did you find a way to call me in Sweden?"*

Minister Tasi was laughing as he said, *"It was easy in Malmo, Sweden, as there is only one Radisson. It was too difficult in Oslo, Norway, as there were many Radissons..."*

While we were talking, God already confirmed I was in Sweden to receive this call and to extend my time in London, so, I agreed to remain in London and assist the Ambassador for the Kingdom of Tonga so the African and Island Nations could receive better standing and recognition within the Global Economic Summit.

God's orchestration causes me to stand in awe. We do serve an awesome God!

Since Minister Tasi stated the Ambassador was not going to be available for a week, I discussed with my witness and we prayed. God confirmed the week would be required for the next phase of our journey.

Required? Yes, that was the full extent of the message, *"Required."*

It was a new assignment being scheduled or should I say squeezed in, 'in between' since God wanted me to go to where the revival broke out in England, to find the home and church of the international evangelist and preacher Smith Wigglesworth.

Oswald Chambers *"Living a life of faith means never knowing where you are being led."*

Kenneth Copeland *"Obedience is an act of love and faith."*

Kathryn Kuhlman *"It is through the Holy Spirit empowering Christ's body of believers, His Church, with power for service that the Father is glorified again and again."*

Chapter 18 In Search of Wigglesworth

I called a fellow prayer team member in London to check on travel arrangements. He was so excited to hear a few details about our current and our next journey. He wanted to become a witness to these days so he added his name to the itinerary for our next phase of the 'Faith Walk.'

So excited in fact, he kept forgetting that he asked me many times for the location. Each time I had to give him the same answer, *"I do not know."* He had no clues to help us find the home and church of Wigglesworth, either.

I wanted to say I would ask a pastor, but, God stopped me.

God was clear about not asking any of the pastors because God wanted to guide me on this journey, so all I could say is the name of the town God told me to travel to while we were sharing the phone call and praying: Newcastle. It seemed odd as this was the town where God orchestrated details for seven weeks in Australia. However, God clearly confirmed Newcastle as the town for our travel destination in England.

The man arranged and confirmed three train tickets to take the Royal Scotsman to Newcastle within moments of our call.

London to Newcastle, England

God is so wise! If I would have asked anyone and everyone or researched anything about everything (which I would have done, thoroughly, prior to venturing out the door!), but relying on Sheila logic would have caused me to miss nearly 100% of what God had 'in store' for us on this journey to find the location of the revival in England, and the church and pastor's residence where Wigglesworth was filled with the Holy Spirit!

Personally, I can highly recommend that when you get the opportunity to travel the countryside of England, you enjoy the Royal Scotsman mode of transportation! We enjoyed the time, in amazing seating, while updating the man from the prayer team about our journey to Norway and Copenhagen and Sweden. The time flew by!

When we arrived in Newcastle, I was not able to resist, as I had no idea how to proceed. I began my 'Sheila inquiry' phase. I asked the information desk about Wigglesworth. Nobody could help. So, I asked them to call the library, but, the library information desk staff told them they could not help.

So, I tried my # 3 or Sheila 'Plan C' option and I called a couple of the people in the phone book with the last name Wigglesworth. Each person I called wondered if they were related, but they were not sure. They wanted me to call them back if I found out they were related. However, I was not on a genealogy journey!

So, I stopped trying the Sheila plan and I cried out to God along with my two prayer partners, to show us the way to Wigglesworth.

God directed us to go to the taxi stand and take the next taxi to the Christian book store. We waited for a while, but we did take the very next taxi. Ah, God! The man driving the taxi was interested in trying to help us because he was baptized in the church where Wigglesworth preached. Thrilled, because I trusted the taxi driver would be able to take us right to the church!

Wrong! He had not been in the church since he was a child, and he was not quite sure where the church was located.

He was very interested in becoming part of our journey, however, since he had just lost his mother and he knew it would be important for him to return to the church and become involved. So, he joined us in our efforts as a fellow 'Faith Walker' vs. merely being our taxi driver.

God directed us to the Christian book store. They sold books on Wigglesworth, but, they were not aware of the location, either.

We continued to pray. While we were purchasing a couple of Wigglesworth books, a man entered the book store and heard our conversations about Wigglesworth. He said a teenager made a display at the library, a wall display about Wigglesworth a couple of days ago. He thought the information might be helpful. I turned to ask him a question, but, as quickly as he appeared, he disappeared.

We rushed the short distance to the local library. As soon as we entered the library we noticed the wall display. The entire wall was dedicated to the life and accomplishments of Smith Wigglesworth. It was amazing.

The teenager had titled the work in such a way that he was reminding people they have forgotten what God did in their area, and they should not forget.

The library staff was not aware of the teenager's work. The information desk is very close to this display. Library staff pass by the wall display as they enter the library each day, and as they go back and forth to the bathroom. However, they were not aware the wall display existed.

The supervisor offered the phone number of the teenager's family. I called and spoke to the teenager's father. He was amazed his son had put together the chronological summary at the library in the past three days, as God asked him to do it … it was done that night and he put it up the next day.

So, God made the request of a teenager who carried out His request within three days of our arrival. Aligned with the timing of God's request that I find Wigglesworth's home church, which keeps me in awe of God's orchestration!

The only 'clue' I received was the name of a local town, Sunderland.

It was late in the day, and God had revealed a lot. The next step would need more prayer in time, so I told the taxi driver that we should go to our hotel and if he would be available, we would like him to be our taxi driver the next morning. He agreed.

The three of us 'from afar' sharing this amazing journey agreed to meet 30 minutes before the taxi driver arrived, so we would have time to pray together.

Before sunrise, God started sharing scriptures with me about the gates in the East being open for us, plus He directed me to scriptures confirming a tithe of all, none of which meant anything to me at the time. However, I shared the details with my prayer partners and witnesses. We prayed, and it was very clear that something about gates in the East would become significant as the day unfolded.

Sunderland, England

We enjoyed the travel with the taxi driver, especially since our journey was bringing him back to his childhood roots in the local church. He spent some time researching Sunderland and he had a couple of ideas where the church might be located. The first church he took us to included an inscription honoring the pastor of Wigglesworth, Alexander Boddy, but, it did not have gates.

When I mentioned the fact God was talking to me about the Eastern gates being opened to us, prior to sunrise, the man lit up like a Christmas tree! He said, *"Probably two gates to the place then, wouldn't you say?"* I smiled and said, *"Probably ..."*

This fact made all the difference to the driver. He drove with confidence until we reached a church, storehouse and house behind a significant fence, and two sets of gates! The first gates included a significant set of chains with locks and a huge padlock. However, the taxi driver was so excited while he quickly pointed out to us that the gates for the main entrance to the church were locked, but, they are not the Eastern gates to the property!

So, he drove us to the Eastern gates and we were able to open the gates and take photos of the church, the storehouse (for the tithe of all – grain and animals, and a portion of all that was brought to the church for their weekly tithe so all shall be blessed and none shall leave in lack) and the house where Wigglesworth was the plumber, fixing the pipes under the sink for the pastor's wife, Mary Boddy. She laid hands and prayed the in-filling of the Holy Spirit and Wigglesworth began speaking in tongues. Some state he was in the Sunderland Revival when this happened. However, people who knew him personally credit Wigglesworth with the Sunderland Revival as it was due to the Holy Spirit in-filling after prayers with his pastor's wife.

Wigglesworth was not taught how to read as a child. The first words he read were the scriptures. Some say he confirmed God taught him how to read and some say it was his wife, Polly, who taught Wigglesworth how to read. Both examples confirm the book which was used to teach Wigglesworth to read was the bible. He did not allow newspapers in his home. He preferred all reading in his home to be the reading of the bible.

A little story about Smith Wigglesworth: A pastor who went with Wigglesworth to a restaurant in Sydney, Australia per a story shared by Dr. Lester Sumrall, a personal friend of Wigglesworth, in *Pioneers of Faith*[8] shared:

"The (Australian) pastor told me, 'Smith Wigglesworth was here in my city recently ... I took him to one of the fanciest restaurants to have lunch on Sunday. When we came into the restaurant, someone took his coat and hung it up for him. He looked around like an eagle. Only wealthy people ate in this restaurant. Instead of sitting down, he took a fork and began to hit the side of his glass with it. BING! BING! BING! BING!

Everybody stopped eating. When he had everybody's attention, he raised his hand and said, 'Ladies and gentlemen, I have noticed since arriving here that none of you prayed over your food. You resemble a bunch of hogs to me. You just jump in and eat without giving thanks to the One who provided it for you. Bow your heads and I'll pray for you. Wigglesworth raised his hands and prayed for those people. Before we left the restaurant, two families came over and got saved."

Another example, shared within Wikipedia[9] summary of Wigglesworth:

I heard a story about Smith praying for a man that had no feet. He told the man to go to the shoe store. The man did not think it was a good idea but he went anyway. When he arrived, they said they did not think that they could help him. In response he said, "Well if I could wear shoes, what size do you think I could wear?" They looked at him a moment and went and got a size they supposed would fit him. The man stuck the nub of his leg down into the shoe, and a foot grew out into it! Next, he placed his other nub in the other shoe, and that foot grew out too!

If you search You Tube options for Kathryn Kuhlman ORU Mabee Center 1974 10 X 14, you will hear about a young girl who was in the worship meeting two years before with severe club feet since birth. After she received prayer and Holy Spirit touch / transference from Kathryn, she was healed. The mother confirms the doctor who did the surgery for her daughter found two new bones in each foot which straightened out her feet. Kathryn also confirms a key point about revival, also. *"It's not revival, it's restoration!"*[10]

God's Storehouse

Tearful, when God revealed the physical 'storehouse.' Before this day, I had only read the facts in scripture which seemed to counter the process of the church. Now, I was able to see an actual storehouse.

In scripture the people were to bring a tithe of all, of their 'increase' in grain, stock, and produce, from all that was harvested in that week, so there would be 'enough' for the priest/pastor and those in need, especially the widows and the orphans.

If it became too much, if the load was too heavy to bring it to the church it would be OK to sell the tithe offering in the marketplace and bring the money provided from the sale to help provide the needs of the storehouse.

God repeatedly confirmed he has been sharing this same message through me within every church around the world, "***God's Storehouse Principle***" (separate book).

The storehouse used to be alive and well in the churches around the world ... however, it seems to be a process which has stopped or it has been replaced, and the 'storehouses' are no longer built next to the church building, and only cash has been considered 'tithe' from the people. And, per most churches, making a pledge is 'good stewardship' to give the church a tithe of their cash from their full income before it is earned and available to promise let alone pray about and contribute a tithe of their increase, confirming God's blessings and declaring how God has blessed them.

Wow. This removes all of the time with God reviewing the 'blessings / increase' and the options to tithe of who we are and what we have for there are fewer and fewer people raising grains and animals to provide food for the people in need, especially the widows and orphans.

God directed me to the exact scriptures about both the gates & tithe. Amazing! God was providing some intense training!

Edinburgh, Scotland

It was Saturday, and I felt I should be at the church on Sunday, while the notice for Sunday service confirmed it would begin early in the morning.

The Lord added an overnight in Edinburgh, Scotland that evening. We already had our train tickets arranged, so we would have to pray diligently about God's plans and if they included being at Wigglesworth's church on Sunday morning …

Amazing scenery as we traveled the northeast coast of England and on to Edinburgh, Scotland.

More prayer time was required after all of the excitement and social conversation time we shared during prior phases of our journey. We were more reflective, especially after God showed us so much within a few hours during the ***Search for Wigglesworth*** phase of our journey.

Silence was my main mode of communication.

I was taking it all in. I was seeking God's plan and purpose for this portion of the journey, while questioning what could be so important to bring us to Scotland after experiencing so much in the prior 24 hours in Newcastle and Sunderland. Feeling tired was not like me, and I was getting frustrated with the real feeling of being exhausted, and the silence I was expressing and God's silence. However, my witnesses were feeling the same, so I said, ***"Let's be*** *tourists for an hour. Let's go for a walk ..."* and, we walked the main street of the town.

We saw the amazing 180 degree view of the ocean shore, Edinburgh Castle.

We returned to our hotel and agreed to pray and refresh, and meet for dinner in an hour and enjoy a nice, relaxing meal together.

When we gathered together, I opened the conversation with a shy approach since the scenery was so beautiful and we had just arrived. While I was offering the option to return on a train to Sunderland in the morning, arriving at the church at the end of the service ... then, I looked up. Both witnesses were nodding. We had to laugh, because my witnesses held up their notes, and confirmed we each found the area to be amazing, but, each one of us had already checked the train schedules for Newcastle / Sunderland in the morning and the three of us had come to the exact same conclusion!

We were packed and ready to go to the train station, early.

Our energy had returned!

We talked about the 'short trip' to Scotland, and we agreed, the people seemed so sad, almost like they were living 'without hope.' Since my witnesses were feeling this way, I shared words of encouragement, ways to see God in everything. It gave them a boost which was evident as I listened to their evaluations of our time together in England and Scotland while we journeyed back to Sunderland.

During the brief time together I shared the fact the Lord confirmed the similarities ... people have forgotten the sacrifice of life for freedom and the ability to worship freely, as they wanted to in Scotland (Wallace, amongst others) vs. being ruled by and forced to be in one nation and one church, the Church of England or the Church of Scotland.

Vision: Revival, An Event or Everyday Occurrence in Fellowship

Since I know you will realize the depth of this vision, and perhaps you are to become a part of God's plan for these days, I will share the vision God showed me. It was a vision of me standing in a very light and bright place. Lots of lights were shining bright since I was in a hospital, standing just inside at the Emergency room entrance with a view of all the activity coming in from the world.

Ambulances were backed up at the entrance with their back doors wide open. Each ambulance carried what appeared to be an identical 'little white wood church' and I saw each church – laying on a gurney – Doctors were confirming the status of each church having flat lined. Each one of the emergency doctors waited for a different doctor or a team of doctors to show up, to 'revive the church/patient.' Workers were everywhere, but, they were waiting on the expert team, but, before the 'blue cart' team could get to the gurney, more and more ambulances were arriving, but they could not even get near the emergency room doors, since additional ambulances were already lined up at the entrance of the emergency room, and, as each one opened the back doors, it was clear, they were each delivering another church to be revived.

In that moment (I have no idea how long I observed this status) God confirmed, *"This is the condition of my people, the church. This is why I sent you to search for Wigglesworth. The heart is where Christ resides. The Holy Spirit guides in truth, strengthening us where we are weak."*

So, why would we repeatedly go into cardiac arrest? Why would a church flat line, and want someone 'in the world' to be bring revival? Why do the people repeatedly need to be revived, brought back from the dead, again and again?

Either we are listening to the Holy Spirit or the closest counterfeit. We have free will and free choice.

God's word is true. When Jesus ascended, he confirmed the Holy Spirit would come and guide us to do the things Jesus did and even greater things. What happened? We are to be trained and equipped to disciple. We are each supposed to teach the people to seek the Holy Spirit in all they do so he will guide them in their coming and going. We are to hear the hearts of those who fellowship with us. We are to hear how we can bless and encourage each other each time we fellowship together … for we each need the heart and mind of Christ and the guidance of the Holy Spirit to walk in my power and authority.

I was stunned, speechless.

Wow. This is the condition of our church, today. This is how the church is appearing to God, with the health of the church requiring a lot of 'reviving' so it is not possible for those who are 'in need' to see that God is blessing his people and he will bless them through the fellowship with 'fellow believers' – wow. I have no idea how long I remained in his arms, speechless.

Then, I cried out to God: ***Lord, what will it take to remind the people about a region known as Sunderland, England, and help them remember how the people were touched while God sent an illiterate man, Wigglesworth, around the world?***

God Made It Personal

Then, the most breathtaking statement happened when God confirmed his truth to me, He had done the same for me as He did for Wigglesworth even though God sent him without degrees, I had degrees and 'world based' accomplishments, and yet, Wigglesworth agreed to go before planes shortened travel, and while he was without:

1. An auto (much of his travel was before autos existed)
2. Credit cards (his lifetime of work ended before credit cards existed)
3. Debit cards (his lifetime of work was before banks provided debit cards)
4. A phone … (most of his lifetime work was before phones were available)

And, 'in spite of' Wigglesworth's circumstances, being an illiterate man and having a family to provide for, God sent Wigglesworth to many continents, also!

God stopped me in my tracks!

God had given me a lot to think about in a very short period of time. God has launched me, globally, as God launched Wigglesworth, and Wigglesworth blessed millions before phones and planes. Ah, God's mighty orchestration.

This vision seemed too big to imagine I could do something about it but I promised God I will teach the truth and I pray each time I teach one they will put their faith into action and teach one so the truth will not fade from their memory.

I cried out to God to show me what he would have me do and help me figure out how to do it, and while I continued the 'rant' God took me back to the meadow, back to the moment when I was four and marching in the meadow. Once again, I heard myself saying, **"I *will do anything you want me to do!*"**

Then, God simply responded, ***"I am with you. I will not forsake you."***

Ah, yes. God had to remind me at 40 what he had confirmed with me at four.

Sunday Church Services in Sunderland, England

Blessed. God delivered us at the church steps as the parishioners were leaving. I was just telling my witnesses that today is a 'New Day' in the church, as we entered. The two female caretakers of the church were going to remove the communion cup but I asked them if they would please wait until we speak to the pastor. My witnesses pointed to a banner over our heads, which was directly above the baptismal fount, 'New Day.' I smiled and said, **"God knows how to make His point!"**

My witnesses spoke to the caretakers, as I spoke with the pastor. By the way, she goes by the name of Pastor Day, since her last name is Day. She was blessed to have us share a few details with her, and she was honored when God confirmed I was to serve communion to her. Then, she served communion to each of us.

Pastor Day offered to drive us to the train station, as she wanted to hear more details about our 'Journey to find the church and home of Wigglesworth.' As she dropped us off at the train station, she confirmed it is a 'New Day' in their church, now that we have shared the info with her, and she is a 'New Day' pastor!!!

God is good to each of us, especially when we 'Faith Walk' together!

1 Corinthians 2:4-5. *And my speech and my preaching were not with persuasive words of human wisdom, but in demonstration of the Spirit and of power, ^{5} that your faith should not be in the wisdom of men but in the power of God.*

Pastor Day, *"I thank God for sending you to our church this morning, for serving communion to me, and for renewing and restoring me for the call upon my life."*

Chapter 19 Kingdom Business, International Spiritual Warfare Conference

God provided. I've got the power suit & I'm ready to go! Wrong! God confirmed I should issue a business card to people, so we could stay in touch with each other. I had the lap top computer, but I did not have a printer, and we would be leaving shortly.

As I prayed, the phone rang. My hostess was gone, but she expected an important call and wanted me to answer the phone. When I did, a man stated he is the owner of a computer company. It sounded like a typical sales call, but, in a British accent, so I laughed, while I told him I was only answering the phone to receive a call my host family was expecting.

When he heard my voice, he laughed and said, *"Are you the American speaking in local churches?"* I was shocked! I responded, *"Yes."*

He said, *"I wondered how I could get in touch with you. I have a printer you can use, and it's yours if you will pay the taxi fare for me to send it to you."*

So, I asked him, *"How much?"* He said, *"…about 15 quid, I imagine."*

So, I called the man and witness from the journey in search of Wigglesworth to ask him about quid and how expensive that might me. He laughed, since as our American dollar is sometimes called 'a buck,' he thought I would know a British pound is often called 'a quid.'

I shared the details. He was so shocked to hear the news he said he would get on the underground to arrive before the taxi arrived, to be a witness to these details. He arrived within seconds of the taxi, and, since I did not have 'quid,' he paid the driver for the printer delivery! Wow. Timely option to help me make business cards for my journey.

Birth of the Ministry: HIS Best!

The only question was, *"What do you want me to call the ministry, God?"*

God reminded me, that each time he answered my question, *"What am I to do for these people?"* God's response was simple and complete, *"Give them My best!"*

God allowed me to hear the many confirmations in each part of the journey, while I was blessed and acknowledged in various languages around the world, after I had asked again and again, *"...what am I to do for these people?"*

Listening close for God's response, after crying out to God for months, asking God what I should do about the judges behind the scenes in the legal maneuvering and God always responded, *"Give them My best."*

So, I prayed for strength to give the people I thought were 'the enemy,' God's best! I was shaky at first, but, God strengthened me each and every time!

Then, as I traveled to various ministries and churches around the world, meeting with business and government leaders, I asked God what I should give them, and God's header for my assignment was always the same, *"Give them My best."*

This confirmed God was forming the foundation of the current ministry, HIS Best! In fact, when I asked God if it was time to establish the ministry, God caused me to see a sign on the side of a truck, a sentence barely visible due to the faded color of the chipped paint. However, odd as the experience seemed, seeing a truck in the next lane on the freeway, while driving to Los Angeles, the sentence was, *"Establish the foundation for HIS ministry!"*

This is why the title of the ministry became HIS Best! And, since the beginning, I have prayed that everyone I meet will experience HIS Best!

A bit of concern, because if I named the ministry God's Best!, as people would think I'm thinking I'm God's best, and I am just one of the Kingdom Kids on the planet at this time. So, I kept praying. Then, again, God showed me a sign, again, **"HIS Best!"**

So, I made the cards, including only the name of the Ministry and the email address, which had to be a bit different, since the web site name was taken the LORD adjusted the title within email and on the internet to: HISBest4us (Facebook); http://hisbest4us.org. I thought I was done, but, God had a few more details to add: STAND Firm, so that none shall perish, so they will choose life, live it abundantly and prosper! Scriptures were noted. Then, on the reverse, the business card, identical with minor changes: STAND Firm so none shall fail, in Life, Relationships and Business! OK. The cards are ready.

Kingdom of Tonga High Commissioner
The Ambassador's Office, Central London

It was Sunday morning and I was preaching at a satellite church of an international ministry headquartered in London. Immediately after the service, I called the Ambassador's office to leave a message. To my surprise, the High Commissioner Akosita answered the phone!

My first response was to offer her some immediate assistance so she would not have to work on Sunday, but, she cleared up the matter immediately. Her chauffeur passed away during the night. She was in the office to contact his family and make arrangements to handle all details required. Since I was available as of Sunday, she provided the facts and made arrangements for us to meet at her home later that day.

This was amazing because the only phone number I was provided was the number for her office, and it was the perfect number to reach her! She provided her home phone number so I could give it to the pastor and the man from the prayer team, the man who purchased the printer for a few quid after becoming a witness in the search for Wigglesworth in Newcastle and Sunderland, England, as we were going to be holding business meetings the next week.

Time with the Ambassador was private. We did not meet with staff, as she was preparing for the Global Economic Summit.

How blessed I am, to realize how valuable the information was for the Ambassador, while she was in the midst of her diligent preparation to represent for their section of the Global Economic Summit, the Caribbean and Pacific Islands, and the African Nations, recognized as one nation titled: 'The Island Nations.'

When our business was concluded and the Ambassador was preparing to leave for the summit, I met with her about my flight arrangements to return home. I was not aware her budget had changed due to former staff returning to Tonga for the State Funeral of the Prince, while I was in Tonga, and the added costs and expenses due to the loss of her chauffeur. Her department budget would not be able to cover the cost of my flight, however, she said I could remain in her home until my flight to America was arranged

Her situation was understandable. And, I am not to look to man for my provision.

Sounds like I understood in the moment, and I was immediately 'at peace,' right? Wrong!

Now, God had some splainin' to do! This is not how it was supposed to be. Scripture confirms a worker is worth their hire.

Needless to say, for the next few hours, I was marching the hallway (my room was on the top floor of the Ambassador's home – and, I was the only guest on that floor). I was seeking a real answer to my real situation!

I was having a major 'human upset' conversation with God… serious then, but, laughable later, since I was telling God about my status, as though God was not aware of my current situation from the moment I had agreed to remain in London … but, now, reality had set in … I have a ticket 'in hand' that will not be valid until mid-October, and it is the end of May.

At midnight, I was so exhausted from my tirade, I simply said, **"God, you are my travel agent. I'm going to bed."** Wish I would have remembered this truth before midnight.

Before 8 AM I thought I heard the staff calling my name, but, I was in the shower, trusting I did not hear the words 'in the natural,' because, after all, who would call me before 8 AM, except God? And, nobody has the home phone number for the Ambassador except the pastor.

Within moments, one of the staff members started banging on the bathroom door. *"Urgent, Ms. Holm, you have an urgent call."*

The prayer team gentleman, a prayer partner and witness to Sunderland and Edinburgh, Scotland was on the phone.

God woke him at midnight. He knew it was urgent to arrange for my flight ticket. He obtained the number from the pastor because he had a meeting at 8 AM, and he had already called his travel agent. He knew if the flight was arranged in seven days and it was round trip vs one way it would be the best option. So, he hoped I could arrange a flight time at least seven days from that date.

OK. I was in total shock, but, it was so like God to extend my stays another seven days. So the question is what is God up to? Clearly, I asked for this flight ticket, however, a round trip ticket, and a delay of seven days?

Silly me, I asked God, *"What do you want me to do in London for seven days?"* as God was saying *"Yes"* to the man through me, and the ticket was being arranged and delivered within the hour.

In awe of what God just did, I remained in the family room, next to the phone I had used. I sat down for a moment to let the facts fully soak in, while I simply had to ask God, *"What am I to do for you during these extra days?"*

God said, *"Look up."* So, I responded, *"I'm already looking up to you."*

Then, God said, *"Look up"* again, and when I did, I noticed a TV screen which showed the God Channel announcement for an International Ministry Spiritual Warfare conference scheduled for the entire week, the entire seven days.

And, God had an extra surprise in store. The next photo on the screen was the special singer I met in Dallas, Earl Harrigan.

OK. I had to laugh. God arranged for Earl Harrigan to come to England to be the featured singer for the conference in London. Ah, how awesome is this God we serve!

And, the work with the Ambassador became the foundation for me being appointed by the International Director of Business for the United Nations as a Business Advisor for under developed nations! It is merely a title, since no work was arranged by or paid for by the United Nations. All of my work with the nations and all provision is God orchestrated!

International Spiritual Warfare Conference
Earl's Court, London

Excited. It was a delightful afternoon to surprise Earl Harrigan while he was rehearsing with the sound crew for the evening meetings. Hard to express how much fun it was to say (while trying to lower my voice to sound a little more like his friend Big John Hall), *"What are you doing in my town?"* Earl was shocked, and he enjoyed my humor! The ministry staff arranged for me to have a front ministry seat, and I was thrilled.

Voodoo Princess
Attempts to Curse Me Off the Planet

The first night, a unique woman sat next to me. She continually disrupted the service. Of course, she chose to do this, while I was trying to enjoy the song Earl was singing.

I kept praying, but, she continued to be disruptive to the entire front rows of the meeting. God confirmed, *"She does not belong in the meeting."* I told the security staff. They noticed she was wearing a badge, so they said she does belong in the meeting.

After the service, the woman was marching the perimeter of the building. I mentioned the details to the security staff, and I confirmed again that God said she does not belong in the meeting. They said, *"If she returns tomorrow night, just point her out to us and we will talk with her."*

The next night, the very minute she arrived she asked me if she could sit next to me again. I told her it had been very disruptive the night before and I really wanted to hear my friend sing tonight, so, I pointed her out to the security staff since they said that was all I had to do and they would talk with her.

But, they told me I would have to walk her to the director of security. So, I did. I kept praying as we walked. The security director wanted me to show him what she was doing the night before. I told him I'm not going to act out what she does. It was clear he did not want to deal with the situation, so, I told him, *"God said she does not belong in the meeting."*

He asked me for proof. So, as I continued to pray, I said, *"Ask registration."*

When he checked, he found out the woman was not registered for the meeting. Registration handed her a badge and she wrote her name on the badge due to the fact she was disrupting the entire entry area of the meeting the first night so instead of the registration staff speaking with her, they merely let her enter.

Security did not want to take action, so I said, *"God help me!"*

God prompted me to face the woman directly and hold my arms up to protect the hearts of the security guards. God directed me as I spoke directly to the woman, *"Since our Lord is confirming you do not belong in this meeting, I'm asking you if Jesus is your Savior?"* She smiled and coyly and pleasantly said, *"Yes, Jesus."*

The director of security is busy confirming she was quoting scripture to him. I kept praying, as I needed direction from God about this and God confirmed, again, she does not belong in this meeting. So, I asked God for the words, and God showed up powerfully!

Through me, God said, *"Who is the closest counterfeit? Does he reside in you?"*

She lunged toward me and her face became contorted, as though she was pressed, hard, against a large partition (Jesus and the angels) between us, but, she was not able to speak, and she did not have a voice … she was muted.

Frozen, nothing was moving, not my lips or my mind! Then, I heard God say, open your mouth, so I did! Then, I was saying, ***"I'm a favored representative of my Lord and Savior Jesus Christ and anything you want to say unto him, you can say to me now."***

Again, she lunged toward me, but she was stopped, hard and fast, by Christ as the invisible barrier between us.

Her face became contorted, again, and she was unable to speak.

So I asked her, ***"If you choose to be in the meeting, you can choose Jesus Christ as your Savior and remain in this place. But, if you do not choose Jesus Christ as your Savior, you must depart from this place. If you choose Christ you will be assisted and supported by everyone here. So, the question is: Do you want to choose Christ now, be free in your life, and remain in the meeting?"***

She reared back, rose up high, and spat at me.

Her spit was stopped by the invisible partition between us. As witnesses we could see it dripping down but it was not able to get to me.

Then, I said, ***"If you do not choose Christ as your Savior to stay in the meeting then you must leave but, these men will be gracious with you and escort you to the door. My prayer is that you will choose Christ and stay but, you have to declare your choice in your own voice as the choice is yours."***

She reared back and in a full, deep and loud guttural voice as many have shared Satan sounds she said, *"He who curses me shall be further cursed!"*

At that very moment, the security director said, *"OK then, she has made her choice."* Immediately, he directed security staff to quickly escort her out of the building.

Then, they received reports that she started marching the perimeter of the building, so they walked her to the train station, and they remained with her until her train arrived.

The security guards wanted prayers after she had left the building. They wanted me to remove any curse, anything she may have spoken over them and I was honored serve, to pray with them and provide the truth: A Christian church is built upon the prophets and apostles with Christ as the chief cornerstone!

The men were completely unaware of the fact that the woman, even though she attends a church in London, and she says the name Jesus, and she actually quotes scripture, she is not a follower of Christ. Instead, she is attending a Satanic based church. Most of the men knew the location of her church since it was located very close to their churches. They did not know the congregation which took over the church building was not Christian. Prior to this night, they were grateful a church was established in the building since the prior congregation was not being able to cover their monthly lease.

By the way, I should mention this fact. The entire group of security guards and the security director were pastors and senior pastors of local churches.

God introduced me around London in one short moment in time. And, God brought the truth to light about what we are dealing with in the world, ***"...we do not wrestle against flesh and blood, but against principalities, against powers, against the rulers of the darkness of this age, against spiritual hosts of wickedness in the heavenly places."*** Critical to put on the full armor of God!

Luke 21:12-19 confirms: ...You will be brought before kings and rulers for My name's sake. ^{13} But it will turn out for you as an occasion for testimony. ^{14} Therefore settle *it* in your hearts not to meditate beforehand on what you will answer; ^{15} for I will give you a mouth and wisdom which all your adversaries will not be able to contradict or resist. ^{16} You will be betrayed even by parents and brothers, relatives and friends ... ^{17} And you will be hated by all for My name's sake. ^{18} But not a hair of your head shall be lost. ^{19} By your patience possess your souls.

God's sense of humor, again, with the business man being told to delay the departure seven days; trusting my work in London was already done, but, God had one more assignment for me, an assignment I had no idea how to do or one word to say until the moment arrived.

What God needs to do through us is beyond human comprehension. We are not to lean on our own understanding. And, God has confirmed again and again in scripture the Holy Spirit will guide us, speak through us, for we merely need to be willing to surrender all to God, to be an open vessel yielded to God's purpose and plans and God will do the rest!

Never would I have been able to imagine anything beyond staying in London and being blessed to hear my friend sing while I enjoyed being with God's people. However, God had me remain and attend a spiritual warfare conference to be the expression of God's ability to work through us and do spiritual warfare when it is required.

Ephesians 2:8-9. For by grace you have been <u>saved through faith</u>, and that not of yourselves; <u>*it is* the gift of God,</u> [9] not of works, lest anyone should boast.

C Nuzum *"Faith is the hand with which we take from God. When we have met all the conditions and taken what God is offering us, we must believe that we have that thing."*

(Beginning of a special sermon by C Nuzum) *In I Timothy 6:12 we are commanded to fight the good fight of faith, and this shows us that just as soon as we believe what God says, an enemy will rise up against us, because we do not fight anybody except enemies. Of course, this enemy is Satan, but he comes in so many ways that we do not always know that it is Satan. The Bible says he will sometimes make himself appear as an angel of light in his efforts to deceive us and get us to accept his lies. But we must never accept or believe anything that does not fully and entirely agree with God's Word. At once the fight begins, and we must not stop until we drive the enemy back. God has promised that He will always cause us to triumph in Christ, but we have to do the fighting. We can draw all the strength we need from God, who says He is a present help in every time of need. Another verse in the Bible (2 Tim. 2:3) tells us to be soldiers and a soldier never goes out to fight without taking an instrument to use to fight with. God is good and considerate and He has given us a weapon to fight with and tells us it is the Word of God and that it is as quick and powerful as a two-edged sword, and yet sharper than any sword. God has given us a weapon that will always win the victory if we will always be good soldiers and never fail to use this mighty weapon.*

Chapter 20 God's Orchestration to Become God's Witness

Conference for Prophets

God blessed me with prayer time with each of the speakers and prayer partners I had met over the past few months, while attending a conference for Prophets. Again, God sends three women to provide prayer support, free transportation to and from the conference, and introductions to pastors attending the conference. God is good!

During a special session with a new speaker, Kingsley Fletcher, I was deeply touched. He shared a powerful testimony regarding his early years, growing up in Africa, evangelizing in the region at the age of 12 and 13.

He told a story about a woman who lost her husband to the fever and her baby was sick with the fever. So, when she heard about the young boy preaching about Jesus, she walked for nearly four days to reach the region where he was preaching and praying with the people.

One day into the trip, her baby died, but the mother kept walking! She cried out to the Lord to save her son for she would lose everything since women have no rights to land or assets or animals owned by the family if she does not have a husband or a son.

When she arrived, the baby was cold, stiff and gray.

The woman said, **"God would not take my husband and my baby from me, so I brought my baby to you, as I know that God will heal my baby when you pray."**

He confirmed her faith and prayed what she had requested, while confirming **"if it be God's will…"** and, as he continued to pray, he could hear and feel that God was breathing life back into the baby, with the toes gaining their color and the gray fading away to life in the body as the baby filled with the fresh breath of life from God and 'came alive' in front of the people.

Then, he stated, when the baby was filled to overflowing with God's breath, and took his first breath all who were in the midst of the gathering were healed!

The people who were blind saw the baby and were no longer blind, and those that were lame forgot they were lame as they danced and rejoiced, and the poor rejoiced and proclaimed how richly they were blessed, for they were all healed in that moment when the healing of the Lord was evidenced in the baby, and their faith was expressed.

The speaker was so powerful. I wanted to speak to him after the session. However, they immediately continued with the next speaker and there were thousands of people in the room, so I remained in my seat.

The next speaker, Prophet Paul Cain, asked the staff to have Kingsley return to the conference center as God had a word for him.

When Kingsley re-entered the room, Paul stated God gave him a vision of two crowns over his head while he was speaking to us; one from God and the other will be given to him by man and he should accept this crown as it is God's plan…and, Kingsley was emotionally shaken, as he began to respond, while 'choked up' as he was so deeply touched.

Paul described the second crown is the fact that he has been asked to accept the crown as the King of a region in Ghana, W. Africa in August and Christian leaders were telling him to not accept this offer as it will affect his anointing, and therefore, his ability to be a strong Christian leader.

At this moment, the Lord told me I would be at this coronation and be a witness to the Lord's plan for his life. As quickly as I heard God say this, I laughed about the option. How would I be able to save enough money to be in Africa in seven months when I had hoped to visit my cousins during forty-four years as missionaries in the Congo? Since I clearly did not know this man how would I even receive an invitation…?

The details will be shared in a later chapter, but, you can be sure I quickly forgot about the Holy Spirit prompting me in this moment, about being in Africa and being God's witness, until I was on my way to Africa as the coronation was days away. I'll save the glorious details of that adventure with the Lord for another chapter of my *"Faith Walk"* because that trip held a lot more 'in store' for me than merely a trip to Africa!

OK. I'll share some more preparation details with you right now, because it includes another conference and four more churches, so, just for you, here are a few of the secrets about how God got me from America to Africa, without me being able to do anything about it. I was, again, able to do nothing about getting myself to Africa, the travel visa, the shots, the flight, and the costs … it was all "a God thing" … 100%!

Christian Leadership Conference, Meetings,
Traveling 1200+ miles with God on One Tank of Gas!

Conference for the church leadership was being held in Northern California, and I was invited by a pastor to meet at the conference the next day! I was hesitant. I had to tell him I would have to rent a car …and more than two tanks of gas … but, he was not worried, because God told him to bless me beyond the rental car for the week and the gas to drive to Northern California (Santa Rosa, above and beyond San Francisco).

God shared the same vision with us during our time at the conference. It was about the war room, the strategy sessions, the leadership needing to come together, to unite, to make plans and to prepare…God even included the exact same furniture in the war room in each of our visions, so we would easily be able to confirm that God wanted us to meet and hold strategy sessions! I was excited --- beyond measure!

The days of the conference were a blessing, and yet, they were jam packed! I met special Christians during each session. But, the man I was supposed to have special meetings with did not have time so we did not strategize.

When I arrived at the hotel to take him to the airport, he was gone. He took an earlier flight. I was stuck. I was leaving, without the promised financial blessing.

When I started my car, I realized the gas tank was empty. I would need at least 2.5 tanks of gas just to get home. I was not happy and I had no option to buy gas. I spent every moment in prayer! The miles 'flew by' while I drove crying and praying the entire way through the town while my gas tank indicator was going from empty to full.

The gas tank indicator confirmed the gas tank was completely full the moment I got to the freeway but I was too busy crying and complaining to God to realize the gas tank went from empty to full!

The prayers were not 'happy' prayers. I was upset. How could God let this happen to me? God heard me cry out for one more confirmation that I was supposed to be at the conference. I needed immediate confirmation and a word of knowledge to gain understanding, as I knew not how God was going to provide the gas for the drive home.

The Holy Spirit prompted me to exit the freeway. The timing was good, as the tears were streaming down my face making it nearly impossible to see the freeway, anyway. When I pulled off at the designated exit, I was thrilled God wanted to talk with me however, there was not a gas station or convenience store or a fast food drive thru. Seemed impossible, but, God had to remind me I had no cash to stop. So, I should not have been surprised that God would find an exit where there was only a business building and a large parking lot. It was a busy parking lot as I pulled off the freeway, but, while God guided me to a parking space, I did not see any people or one car!

So, even in this situation, when I was asking for answers, again, I was asking if I really needed to pull off the freeway, God immediately stated He needed my full attention and I needed to write down what He needed to tell me.

Quickly, I looked through the luggage in the front seat for a notepad and I wrote down the statement God shared, "***Not enough of my men are preparing and putting on their steel toed boots to*** *march with Me, so I am having to call forth my women, even my widows and my orphans, to prepare my Army to march with Me before the SONrise."* Then, God confirmed that I was supposed to share this exact message with the speaker and pastor the moment I returned home.

I'm not sure how long the tears flowed. It was July and I have no idea how long I sat in the car with the air conditioning off, but God took care of me!

When I was ready to get back on the road again, people and cars were everywhere as I drove out of the parking lot.

As I entered on to the freeway, I noticed the gas tank was still full!

God brought me home on the same tank of gas. Only God kept the tank full!

I called the pastor and speaker. I shared the message from God.

He said, "*God shared a vision confirming where (he) is satisfied as the mouse to the elephant, to gnaw on the ankle, but, God showed him that when I bite the ankle and the elephant does not respond, I run up the elephant's leg. Then I swing on the tail, and since I have not gained the attention of the elephant, and he does not respond or move, then I run up to the left ear and shout, and, I run to the right ear and shout, until I get the elephant to move.*"

He said the elephant is the body of Christ and that I do get it to move. He said this vision was a confirmation that we are to meet, again and I was thrilled, because it was true for me, as God confirmed the message exactly in the moment while he was stating it!

I returned to an invitation to be in meetings on the Central California coast, which would typically require more than two tanks of gas. While I was ready to tell the person I would have to arrange for gas, God was already saying "*Yes*" through me, as I heard my voice responding "*Yes.*" I was immediately re-packing to be gone for two to three days.

The speaker I enjoyed so much at the Prophets Conference in January, Kingsley Fletcher, was going to be speaking at these meetings.

The evening session with Kingsley as the speaker were as special as the moments in January. He was surrounded after his talk, so God told me to give him my ministry business card and request the Covenant tapes which were not available.

A host family provided housing for the days of meetings. The next morning (fourth morning in the region), my pager started notifying me of calls by 7:30 AM. Since I was new to the host family, I did not want to bother them before 8 AM, and it was difficult to wait, since the pager noted numerous phone numbers and messages from various numbers by 8 AM.

It was Kingsley. He was awakened by the Lord prompting him to open his bible, pull out my card, and pray over my name at 6 AM. He had not 'settled in' until about 3 AM, since he met with pastors and friends after the evening service. God has a sense of humor!

Kingsley knew God wanted us to speak, so he invited me to a church that evening. Again, I hesitated, since it would typically require another tank of gas. However, God was saying, "***Yes, I'll be there***" through me, before I could even make a comment about the gas tank.

A tank which was still full!

We met briefly at the end of the evening but, he was out of time. He said we would meet another time and he would keep praying. I was in a serious 'in my head' discussion with God about not being in Ghana, West Africa in three weeks, and yet, in this moment God said to me "...***tell him you will talk with him in Ghana***" I actually said, "***I will not be in Ghana!***" out loud.

The man smiled and said, "***You do not have to come to Ghana to speak with me, we can speak over the phone, or God will make arrangements for us to talk soon. I have a ministry in the US...***"

Well, God immediately dealt with me, as soon as I was in the rental car and headed to the home of my host family!

God confirmed, again, I would be in Ghana and I would be God's witness.

God's Provision at Warp Speed

The host family asked me to stay another night and join them for a church service. The meeting included a special couple who were directed by God to sit next to me. The man leaned over and asked, *"You are in ministry?"* I nodded. He handed me an envelope which God told him to prepare earlier in the day.

After the meeting, they asked a few questions and I shared a few details. They were thrilled to hear about what God was doing. The man did not know that God had provided for an extension of time for me to be in the meetings the past few days before I resolve the rental car payment. The man was blessed when he found out the blessing in the envelope was exactly the amount I needed to resolve the rental car. He had tears as he confirmed it was exactly the amount God wanted him to prepare and bring with him to the church service to contribute. And, I could take a breath, as God was keeping the gas tank full, still!

Smith Wigglesworth *"Great faith is the product of great fights. Great testimonies are the outcome of great tests. Great triumphs can only come out of great trials."*

Psalm 20:4-5. *May He grant you according to your heart's desire, and fulfill all your purpose. [5] We will rejoice in your salvation, And in the name of our God we will set up our banners! May the Lord fulfill all your petitions.*

Chapter 21 God Fulfills a Lifetime Dream ... My Feet on the Soil in Africa!

Three Weeks before Africa

God arranged for me to be in Ghana within three weeks.

Remember the lap top Pastor Harald Dewberry left with me in Australia? Finally, I was home long enough to make arrangements to meet with him and return it to him.

When I prepared to leave his office, he handed me a piece of paper. I was surprised, but, he said, "*God prompted me to give you this because you have been here a few times to bless us and we never took you to lunch.*"

God immediately confirmed the check is for the trip to Africa. God was directing my steps. The trip was taking place in three weeks. I finally called Kingsley Fetcher's church office to check on the details for the trip.

The travel visa required a fee and a series of shots. The shots should have been arranged 30 days in advance. God confirmed it is being arranged, so I obtained the visa application to submit the records in time. God knew a Doctor at the local clinic (about a 15 minute walk from my home) and directed me to meet with him. The Doctor has a unique practice. He has the only serums available to prepare rescue teams who must depart with little or no notice! This is something I did not realize existed, but God!

God was putting the trip together, step by step, with each fee being supplied by the source God arranged and the provision was in the exact amount needed. God confirmed the payment for the visa to be in Ghana, the flights to join the group in Miami for the final flight to Ghana, and the fees for the hotel and meals in Ghana were going to be supplied by selling the Christian scarves which I sell when I speak.

God prompted me to pencil out the remaining costs for the trip.

OK. I needed to sell eight dozen scarves.

God directed me to call the manager of the Christian bookstore within the National Prayer Center (established by C Peter Wagner and his wife, Doris, Chuck Pierce and Bobbye Byerly), which is located within the same parking structure as the Conference of the Prophets I attended at the beginning of this journey seven months before. The conference center is the former church of Pastor Ted

Haggard, the man who received the vision for the National Prayer Center and gathered the people together to make it happen.

The manager said she would place an initial order of five-dozen.

Personally thanking her, while I was praying fervently, reminding God I need to sell eight dozen if this is how God is going to pay for the visa plus the trip.

Then, the manager stated, "... *five dozen might not be enough."* I asked if she wanted ten or twelve dozen, but, to my surprise in that moment she said, "...*eight dozen...that is what I need. I want to start with an order of eight dozen."*

Ah, God's sense of humor, exactly what I needed, and not an extra coin (cent)!

Since I did not have a bank account, yet, I asked the manager if she would mind helping me by sending the payment directly to a ministry on the opposite coast, North Carolina on the East Coast. She asked about the details. This was God's orchestration, the opportunity for me to confirm with her how she had helped me with this new testimony. The manager was pleased. She agreed to send the check to the ministry.

God paid for everything required for the trip within 3 days.

My trip to Africa was arranged within 72 hours, after I did not arrange anything during the past seven months. Everything was paid for and arranged without my involvement. Not one coin passed through my hands. We do serve an awesome God!

As you can see, I do not control the flow of God's provision!

As God confirmed time and again by providing exactly what was needed within the currency exchange rate of each nation, God made the message simple and clear. I do not travel on 'my currency' when I travel with God. I travel on God's currency.

One Week Prior to Africa

Attending a local Lutheran Church, the week prior to my trip, a woman in the church heard I was going to Africa and she handed me $100 for my journey.

Great! I trust this is how God will provide for the African outfit required for the coronation!

Each participant is required to dress in African attire for the coronation, so I was thrilled to know I would have the cash to purchase the African outfit!

On the Soil in Africa

Blessings & Blessings & Blessings…More than a coronation!

A national Christian conference was underway.

TD Jakes was on the platform! It was his first trip to Africa, also.

The program was being translated into many dialects and languages for the participants filling the conference hall, the balcony levels, and every inch where they could stand and hear the message!

Kingsley Fletcher spoke to the people in many of the Africans dialects. The people cheered when he spoke in the dialect of their region.

Only three nights of 'sleeping', within the week I was 'on the soil' in Africa and that is all I needed because God's plans and the work he does through me energizes me. That's how I can quickly tell the difference between what I'm doing:

1. Serving God's people, according to God's plan and purpose, or if I am

2. "Sheila-tizing" a situation, feeling tired and exhausted. (you can feel free to insert your name to confirm to you which version of the plan you are participating in at any given time while proceeding upon an assignment).

God's plans energize me. My plans tire me out. This is true even when I'm not on a specific assignment. When I 'check in' on the current state of affairs, a.k.a., how I'm feeling, I know in an instant which plan I am operating within!

Days of prayer sessions, late into the evening/morning! Nights with less than three hours to sleep became nights of prayers in the lobby of the hotel, so my room-mate would not be disturbed.

The first night, they held a fashion show. The outfits were amazing, but, they started at $150 dollars, so I was not able to think about any of them as an option for the coronation. My daily prayer: **Lord, you did not bring me all the way to Africa to not be** *able to attend the coronation as your witness, so I thank you now for the African outfit you are going to provide!*

A bit of personal, Africa history: After writing to my cousins, missionaries in the Congo for 44 years: 1. Beginning before it became Zaire, 2. Surviving the coup d'état while being detained / imprisoned, 3. Remaining after the country returned to the Democratic Republic of the Congo. When the next take-over occurred, they decided 44 years was a good retirement point. They left America after they were married in the 50's and they were only home for brief furloughs. It was a dream (aka, a bucket list item) from the first moment I could send them a picture and a few words on the thin, light blue airmail paper sheet.

God knew I had always wanted to be with them in Africa, even if it was for just a little while! Being drawn to be in Africa for decades, it was impossible to comprehend at first that God had arranged for this special trip within a few days and the trip was already unfolding before the reality of the magnitude of this trip started to soak in.

The people, the faith they possess! It was amazing to be 'on the soil' in Africa.

African Time

There I was, in the front seat of the bus every morning. That is where anyone could find me, whether there was time for breakfast or not. I did not want to miss one moment of this trip! As the days passed, it became comical to realize that 8 AM departure time was 'a plan' - but, in African time - not a reality, as everyone soon learned. The bus may be leaving at 9 or 10:30 AM or noon if you base the trip on actual departure times. All we knew was, the brochure said the bus was scheduled to leave at 8 and it would leave at some point. Typically that point in time was long after 8 AM!

Only four of us went to the youth concert on Saturday night, but, that number of participants provided for transportation to be arranged. The concert, the talent, the energy of the youth and the performers praising God, it was a fabulous night!

Sunday, after I kept God busy most of the night because as God already knew nobody was making arrangements for any of the tour group to be in a church on Sunday morning; the people wanted to sleep in and get some extra rest due to the amazing coronation within the tribal region followed by an evening dinner and celebration. Sunday morning they were preparing for the consecration service at Bishop Duncan Williams' (footnote number 11) church in Accra. This is why the tour bus will not be going and they are not arranging a van or a car for just one person!

My prayer included the beginning of the mantra: **Lord, you did not bring me all the way to Africa to not be able to attend a church service, so I thank you now for making the transportation arrangements you are going to provide!**

As I laid my head down to sleep, I prayed to the Lord my soul to keep AND that God will wake me and help me get to the church on time!

OK. You know me by now! I didn't stop there. I applied a bit more pressure!

I reminded God a few times that he would not bring me all the way to Africa, and then, have me be in a hotel room in Africa on a Sunday, and not bring me into a church with his people. God really listened! God made all of the arrangements, while I rested.

God woke me exactly in time to prepare. Then, God told me exactly when to go to the lobby. God corrected me this time since I always took the stairs, but, God wanted me to take the elevator, so, after he reminded me a second time, I obeyed!

As I came out of the elevator, I saw a man walking toward the elevator with the most beautiful layers of white satin robes. God brought him to my attention and told me to tell him I admired his robes. So, as he passed by me I told him, *"**Beautiful robes.**"*

Then, as I continued to walk past him toward the lobby, the Holy Spirit clearly corrected me as God evidently trusted I would say more. God knows me! God told me he sent that man for me, so I needed to turn around and ask the man, *"**Are you going to church?**"*

To this day (since we have stayed in touch, and I flew to London to attend his ordination as a pastor), we still laugh about this 'meeting' as I did not say hello or introduce myself, I merely turned around seconds before the elevator door closed, and I said, "Are you going to church?"

He said, "*Yes.*" So, I waited by the elevator doors until he returned! Within moments, he returned with the couple from Jamaica who sang at the conference. They were going to be singing at his church.

He also picked up the UN diplomat. God has a sense of humor!

The car is clearly a very, very small compact. It is barely a four-passenger car so adding me to his car meant five passengers plus a guitar were being squeezed into it. A diplomat in the front seat. I sat in the # 5 (middle of the back seat) position between the singers and that meant that I had to maneuver the guitar so the man God was introducing me to, Pastor Charles Benneh, could actually shift the gears. Ah, the blessings and the sense of humor our Lord possesses!

When I arrived, the senior pastor met me at the office door, Pastor Sam Ankrah. He thanked me for coming to his church. He was involved with the conference, so I thanked him for the opportunity to share a few of the glorious details during these days and to be in his church.

As we entered the church together, I followed Pastor Sam as we angled along the narrow dirt path between the small wooden folding chairs. Sometimes, it caused us to walk sideways since every seat was filled!

The men were wearing long sleeved shirts and ties. They were holding kerchiefs, while they were dancing to the wonderful praise music, and we were moving slowly toward the front, and yet, already dealing with the heat amidst taking in the many blessings!

I was not preaching, but, Pastor Sam introduced me and asked me to share a few sentences that morning. It was a last minute invitation as I told him I would be honored, he had already handed me the microphone.

For the first time, I turned and faced the sea of faces. In that moment it hit me. This would not be as easy as it is each time I'm in front of conference halls around the world. Today it was going to be very different because there I was in the midst of the multitude in Africa, in the front of the church with people who are expressing praise and worship and faith at a level I had never experienced before.

Tears flowed down my face, as I shared about seven sentences with the people. My mind does not remember all of it, while the Lord spoke His promises through me, because I remember saying God's confirmation/answer to my cries over the decades, "*For since I was a young child, I asked my Lord to please send me to Africa, for my cousins were in the Congo as missionaries and each time I folded and sealed their air mail letters, I prayed for God to send me to the Congo. So, I trusted, someday, the Congo would be my destination. However, the Lord confirms in my heart this day that if He would send me to the Congo today, they would not be ready to hear what God wants to say to you, his beloved people in Ghana, which is why God has sent me to you, to be here with you ..."* and the Lord shared a word for the people as the people continued to praise and cheers rang out in the crowd.

Personally, I've not received a copy of the audiotape of this day, so I'm not sure of the exact words or what else was said, and I never remember the word God has for the people, whether it is for one person or a congregation. However, I do know that I was so deeply touched and blessed by the people, before, during and after the moments I shared a few words with them and I pray they are blessed as well.

The faith of the people was so evident, so, I mentioned my observations to Pastor Sam. He told me that the people do not earn $200 per month and their rent alone is $200 per month, so they have to live by faith and know the provision of the Lord will be sufficient to meet their needs. Pastor Charles Benneh gave me a tour of the classrooms for the Discipleship Program the next evening, moments before the evening conference schedule:

Discipleship course: *the people go through a ten-week preparation, discipleship course before they become church members, so they know what their salvation means and how to witness their faith to others. I was deeply blessed by this.*

*Pastor Sam approved for Pastor Charles to let me meet with the instructors and view the ten programs being conducted each Monday evening. It was an added blessing to see the children participate, and to hear the instructor's state: "**The family comes, and learns, and prays, together**" ... praise God!*

The music continued. Then, Pastor Sam stated he and his wife would be honoring the singers at lunch the next day and providing a Ghanaian outfit for them, to share Ghana wherever the Lord takes them in the world.

Applauding them, while I was sharing my agreement and acknowledgment of their music, but, they turned to me and said, **"You are included. You are going to be with us. You are going to receive an outfit."**

Total shock, as Pastor Sam took my hand, and brought me back up to the podium to announce to the people that God has sent a special servant from the West Coast of America to the West Coast of Africa and this is the beginning of a great work the Lord will do through us, because we have come together and aligned to fulfill upon His purpose…and then, he shared a powerful prophetic word over my life…

Pastor Sam, the congregation and the seamstress (more than eight months pregnant) all provided outfits for me. Seven in all, while I was only in Africa for seven days: Royal Blue for the coronation, a Royal Purple with white and gold shells representing the West Coasts, for the consecration service at the church of Bishop Duncan Williams.[11]

Plus, they made a beautiful set of the white satin 'Royal Speaker Robes' with extensive gold stitching, with a purple thread design added, and a white linen set with all gold thread, and a green and gold European suit with a reversible jacket and skirt, which was made to my exact measurements so it qualifies as a pencil skirt, and a casual green travel outfit, and extra pants and tunics for the speaker robe sets. We do serve an awesome God.

We learned an African worship song, a very special and simple message. It was shared by the praise and worship team from Bishop Duncan William's church (footnote 11):

ONE MORE TIME

ONE MORE TIME

HE HAS ALLOWED US TO COME TOGETHER

ONE MORE TIME

By the time we sang the verse for the third time, there was not a dry eye in the house!

We Serve An Awesome God

Another episode of: The rest of the story!

Remember the $100 I received for trip? After offerings and the purchase of one soda per day, I had a little more than $40 in my pocket when I returned home. I was thrilled. It was going to be enough to take a commuter bus to the commuter train so I could rent a car for a day, to run errands, pick up mail and pick up a few groceries.

Well, the rental agency had changed managers and policies!

Now, the woman in charge required a $200 deposit. I was in shock. I was also stuck at the train station a good distance from my home. Since she needed an immediate answer, by the grace of God I heard myself saying, "*...then, there will have to be a check for $160 in my PO Box.*"

Due to my unique situation, the new manager decided to be the one who would pick me up. She immediately demanded the $40 cash before we went to my PO Box.

God provided a check for $164.50. Thrilled due to $4.50 extra to buy some fresh fruit.

She agreed to accept the check, but, she would not refund a penny. She insisted on keeping every cent.

I was feeling upset, but, her decision was final. My status was clear. I drove to the home of my friend to check emails, the woman who purchased the journal before my flight to London a couple of months ago. She let me check emails and she served a meal while I updated her about my trip to Africa.

To my amazement, God had arranged another trip confirmed by email. I had no idea how I would be able to make the next trip. I prayed and God said a ticket was at 'will call' at the airport. I did not even know the airport had a 'will call' ticket option!

I left the car at the airport rental agency location the next morning, and I received the entire cash balance of the $200+ deposit for my next trip. God is good!

I was not able to use the skycap at the airport, as I did not have a ticket 'in hand.' There I was, pulling the luggage through the airport without knowing a thing about a will call window.

As I approached the airlines ticket counter, the woman actually smiled and said: *"I am the will call person for the airline."* I handed her my passport and she handed me the ticket.

Then, she was gone before I could even say thank you.

A separate employee appeared, asked for my flight ticket. She arranged the tags for my luggage.

May each blessing from our Lord be shared with all who have eyes to see and ears to hear. May our journeys with God become a 'faith walk' testimony we share far and wide.

This book may be our first time of coming together.

However, as you repeat the verse, ONE MORE TIME, I'm praying with you and toasting your entry into your 'Faith Walk' … and, I look forward to hearing your testimonies of the work God is doing in your life to bless those who are fortunate to be around you and hear about your journey with God. They will be blessed by you … so, here's to our next ONE MORE TIME! May you remain blessed and experience HIS Best until …

Pastor Sam *"Truly, God has sent you to us with a strong word for our church."*

Pastor Charles *"It blesses my soul to hear of your faith & see the fruit of the ministry."*

Johannesburg, South Africa, Pastor Jhanni *"God is doing a good work through you and I pray with you and our church."*

Aimee Semple McPherson *"You don't need to be an orator. What God wants is plain people with the good news in their hearts, who are willing to go and tell it to others. The love of winning souls for Jesus Christ sets a fire burning in one's bones. Soul-winning is the most important thing in the world. All I have is on the altar for the Lord and while I have my life and strength, I will put my whole being into the carrying out of this Great Commission."*

Epilogue

Skipping back and forth 'across the pond'

God has continued to connect me with pastors from around the world, gathering with them in London. I've been blessed with introductions to top Bishops, worship leaders, singers, and speakers from various parts of the globe during each trip. The testimonies of the host families upon my arrival and then, after we share time together and confirm in the moment what God is saying and doing have been an added blessing.

In fact, the first time God arranged for me to return to London His orchestration was '100% evident!'

Flight Ticket Orchestration,
Still Amazing and Beyond Comprehension

Beyond 'will call tickets,' God was orchestrating flight details.

Remember the one-half of the frequent flyer ticket (return to London)? Well it provided a return flight I was not able to use at that time, due to extending in London.

God was immediately arranging a flight to London prior to October 15, so, as God had arranged in advance, I was able to use the remaining half of the round trip provided by the business man: 'a round trip ticket is the best option, if I would stay in London another seven more days.' So, without an extra coin, God had arranged for me to be able to meet the global leaders and African pastors in London.

But, that is not the full story about how God orchestrates the details.

Timing of Flight Orchestration, Beyond Comprehension

The rest of the story: Host family.

God arranged my flight to London on the exact day when my host family could make arrangements. My hostess had just returned from the hospital after surgery. They deserved time for special prayers and God arranged. The couple was a deep blessing.

God had lifted them up from leaving Nigeria with merely the shirt on their back to arranging for an executive position for him to secure a home and helping her gain a top position in the housing authority so she is helping many families arrange for safe and secure housing throughout London.

The rest of the story: Speaker, last minute because I merely showed up.

Their pastor was away and the scheduled speaker missed his flight, so I was introduced to the church by my host before I knew I was going to speak merely due to sharing the fact with him during our prayer time that I only have to show up as an empty vessel for God to be able to fill me with his words and use me as a speaker.

On the next trip to London, their pastor arranged for me to have a special audio tape copy so I could hear the message God delivered through me. He said it was a special blessing to him, so he searched a few tape companies to find the best quality.

The rest of the story: God blesses me with the message months later.

When I returned to America, I forgot the tape was 'in the car' until God prompted me to stop my little 'pity party moment' to put that specific audio tape into the tape deck.

FYI: My auto is 14 years old so it still has a tape deck. Everyone thinks it is brand new when they see it. God has shown me through the extensive losses in my life that it is an honor to care for all of the provision God arranges and it has been a blessing to have a car once again!

Amazed by God's words: The message God delivered through me 'without notice' months before was the exact word I needed to hear in that moment. So strong, in fact, I had to pull over and park the car for a while because the tears were flowing.

The rest of the story: Healing a heart.

Remember the woman from Australia that moved to London and lost faith in God and his provision?

Well, God prompted me to share the details of my journey with her so I sent her a copy of my ministry newsletter which outlined how God continued to take me country to country, nation to nation after I left her home.

When I returned to London, she immediately sought ways to connect with me. God confirmed in her heart and mine that we were to meet. So, she actually arranged to come to the home of my host family in the East of London – causing her to travel to London and then across town – and she immediately asked me to pray with her that Christ would enter her heart and mind and renew her commitment! We did.

She was introduced to a pastor in London who was visiting with me when she arrived. Since he was in the house, he participated with us in prayer. She has remained in touch with the pastor and she has been on her 'Faith Walk' ever since!

And, I trust God was orchestrating these details from the date he required a round trip ticket from the business man. In fact, I trust the orchestration began during our first phone calls while she lived in Australia.

God is amazing at orchestrating details … in advance of the time when God wants me to 'show up' on his behalf!

The rest of the story: God's introductions continue to amaze.

God has connected many business and church leaders together through additional meetings with Pastor Sam and Pastor Charles from Ghana West Africa during days in London on numerous occasions since our days in Ghana. We have met with his ministry staff. I've attended the ordination of three of his pastors in London. I have introduced them to international pastors and bishops in London and he has introduced me to international pastors and ministries in London, especially to the churches building studios and bible colleges, and to singer and sister Osene.

One of the biggest turnaround introductions was during a first meeting with a special Bishop in London, Bishop John Francis.

I was spending time introducing key pastors I had met during my travels nation to nation, the men I admired who were meeting with me in London. The Bishops were appreciative of the meetings and introductions.

Then, I met with Bishop John Francis who is now featured on Trinity Broadcasting Network (TBN). He took me aside and said, ***"Why are you so busy introducing me to others? What if we miss God's plan and purpose for us to meet and see what he would have us do together?"***

It stopped me in my tracks. What if I was qualified to bless the Bishops?

I've learned, since, when we fully surrender we operate with God's knowledge and wisdom and not upon our own understanding!

God repeats this process in our travels together many times and I stand in awe each time the process unfolds!

God is truly up to something, and we are enjoying the time with our Heavenly Father while the details continue to unfold.

God continued his masterful orchestration and provided seven trips in the next twelve months, confirming introductions to numerous pastors, ministries and international bishops, who were meeting in London at the same time.

God's Currency

A new type of training: ***God's Storehouse Principle.*** More about this in my book of this title while it is critical to realize God never made his plans with the body to be all about money. A tithe is not of the entire income. It is of the increase/blessing and not pledging future cash.

An Example: Each time I flew to Europe, I only a five dollar bill in my wallet. Each time I returned, I noticed I only had the five dollar bill in my wallet.

I wanted to laugh but I also wanted to know how this was possible, so I asked God about it. God laughed, as he confirmed, ***"I'm still trying to show you ... when you travel with me, you travel on my currency ... I do not use your currency ..."*** Tears about what God does in my life, while I am still very human and I may not always realize the full impact of everything He is doing in the exact moment when it happens! I only pray that God continues to use me.

God's Confirming Vision

God showed me that what he wants is me and it is the same for you and as God showed me how my words leave my mouth and touch thousands of lives, far more lives than I can see and recognize, as the words impact the people I see before me, then, they continue to touch each of the people they know and the words impact the lives of their family members and business associates, and their pastors, and friends and prayer partners and each of their lives, and it goes on & on & on & on ...

Trusting you have noticed the pattern in the 'launching forth' opportunities I have shared. God revealed his provision exactly when needed in each region He sent me to!

Each time I was given the next assignment, I was sent without an extra coin or tunic. While I was blessing the people, God was providing each need within the required 'currency' in the region and the tunics of the perfect fabric for that region, and yet, each time I left for the next assignment I went without an extra coin or tunic!

Well, as you can tell, God has been doing the same thing with me ever since, based upon my willingness to be in meetings, blessing pastors and their ministries,. kingdom business leaders and their businesses around the world, by "being available" to share what God is doing on behalf of God's church, while God continues "*A Faith Walk*" by bringing a woman into their midst ONE MORE TIME! May it be the same for you, until the next ONE MORE TIME our Lord brings us together!

Testimonies are the 'all of it' and not just the 'fun and good bits' as my friends in London would say! In 2006, my story was structured into a film script and won a film festival. I thought for sure it would be produced as a feature film within a few months. Instead, I spent a few years learning about the film and TV series industry requirements from writing to obtaining funding, finding production and distribution options. In 2007, my ***Seven Step Business Plan*** with Foreword by Ken Blanchard business book was published in America. The content provided invitations and opportunities to become an instructor within the Buckminster Fuller School for Entrepreneurs. I traveled to Kuala Lumpur, Malaysia, **during Ramadan**, Shanghai and Shenzen, China. In 2008, due to multiple issues with regard to the multiple IDs issued to me, I lost title to my home. In 2009, my business book was published in the Spanish Language, Latin America Edition. In 2010, my business book was added to required books for the European Union Chamber of Commerce curriculum. In 2011, I was not aware of the fact I was removed from the system by the people who promised to protect me / my record. I did not exist! In 2012, I was nearly arrested due to being removed, erased: 2012-2014.

Lord be with me, always, send me where you need me to be in the world, protected by the blood of my Savior, Jesus Christ, while I remain aligned with your will, so your purpose and plan for my life will be fulfilled. Amen. God's plan continues through all of this as I am repeatedly reminded about the daily plan: ***It's a Faith Walk!***

A personal note 'just between us'

I look forward to hearing from you, and hearing your details about the *'Faith Walk'* you are experiencing, or you have experienced! Until we meet, speak and/or email the next ONE MORE TIME, enjoy the journey(s) shared in this book and the journey(s) God is and will continue to take you on! Write to me and share the testimonies of the glorious work our Lord is doing in your life. Until the next ONE MORE TIME our Lord brings us together, as always, HIS Best!

Sheila

Email: hisbest4usorders@gmail.com

Use the Subject Line: *It's A Faith Walk!*

Web site: http://hisbest4us.org

Facebook HISBest4us

Ephesians 2:19-22 *We are no longer foreigners and aliens, but fellow citizens... members of God's household, built on the foundation of the apostles and prophets, with Christ Jesus himself as the chief cornerstone. In Him the whole building is joined together and rises to become a holy temple in the Lord. And in Him you too are being built together to become a dwelling in which God lives by His Spirit.*

II Corinthians 12:14-15. (a) *"Now, I am ready to visit you...what I want is not your possessions but you...So I will very gladly spend for you everything I have and expend myself as well."*

II Corinthians 13:11-14. *Aim for perfection ... be of one mind, live in peace, and the God of love and peace will be with you. May the grace of the Lord Jesus Christ, and the love of God, and the fellowship of the Holy Spirit be with you all.*

FOOTNOTES

[1] 1919 Dare to Believe, Then Command sermon by Smith Wigglesworth as published in the Pentecostal Evangel on March 30, 1940. A complete copy of the sermon is provided following the footnotes.

[2] Lutheran minister, Bredesen became the first ordained clergyman from a mainline denomination to receive the Pentecostal experience of the Baptism in the Holy Spirit, openly tell of his experience and keep his ordination and credentials in a mainline (Lutheran) denomination. In a letter to the editor of *Eternity Magazine*, Harald Bredesen and Jean Stone Williams coined the term "Charismatic Renewal." www.wikipedia.com/harald_bredesen

[3] John Willison, plane crash. Chemical fumes filled lungs of rescue workers; Jesus breathed fresh breath into John; no evidence of chemical fumes in his lungs. Angel & Jesus held back flames until 3rd or 4th rescue worker removed John from inferno which engulfed his plane. All bones broken in jaw as confirmed by X-ray. Jesus healed jaw 'overnight' before surgery. Couple pulled over to pray "No pain." John spoke at a Rotary meeting. Man was in the audience to hear John's testimony: experienced no pain!

[4] Became a champion debater in high school. Thought college debate team was a good option. However, Augustana debate team perished in a small plane crash. My dream died. I vowed to never fly in a small plane.

[5] Ed Silvoso, founder of Harvest Evangelism.

[6] Picture provided aligns with Prophetic word received three months later. John Kelly: "***God showed a vision of (me) as the mouse to the elephant. After persistence, the elephant (body of Christ) finally moves.***"

[7] Rees Howells, intercession, faith and spiritual warfare are possible with the Holy Spirit.

[8] Dr. Lester Sumrall, author or **Pioneers of Faith** and friend of Smith Wigglesworth.

[9] http://en.wikipedia.org/wiki/Smith_Wigglesworth

[10] Kathryn Kuhlman confirms it's not revival, it's restoration. Not by our work or power, by the Holy Spirit.

[11] Bishop Duncan Williams is often featured on TBN. He is positioned on boards of top international ministries. He is the Presiding Archbishop and General Overseer of Christian Action Faith Ministries (CAFM), head-quartered in the capital of Accra, Ghana, West Africa.

[12] Please view the DVD **Monumental** for further details. www.monumentalmovie.com. Kirk Cameron proceeds upon the Pilgrim's journey from England to America. Friends are so deeply touched by **Monumental,** they are buying DVD copies for their family and friends.

http://en.wikipedia.org/wiki/National_Monument_to_the_Forefathers.

Books by Author

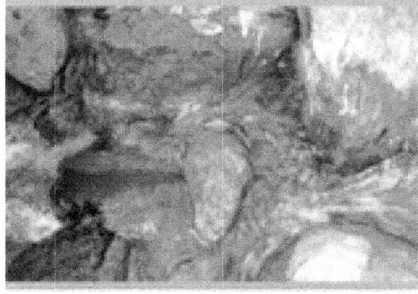

God's Storehouse Principle

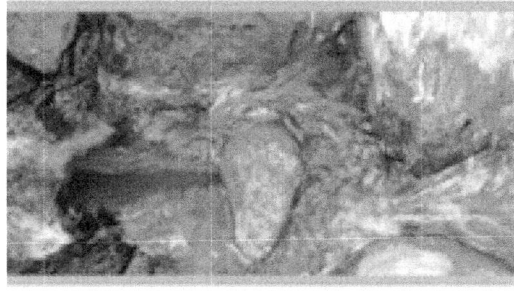

Workbook for God's Storehouse Principle

God's Currency

A Wake Up Call:

It's Restoration Time!

In Search of

Wigglesworth

In One Accord

 A Peculiar People

 Always Speak Life

Christmas

Nation Restoration

Seven Step Business Plan

Latin America edition: Spanish Language, 2009

ACKNOWLEDGMENTS

AFRICA

Ghana, West Africa

Pastor Sam,

> **"Truly, God has sent you to us with a strong word for our church."**

Pastor Charles,

> **"It blesses my soul to hear of your faith & see the fruit of the ministry."**

Johannesburg, South Africa, Pastor Jhanni,

> **"God is doing a good work through you and I pray with you & our church."**

Coronation Ceremony

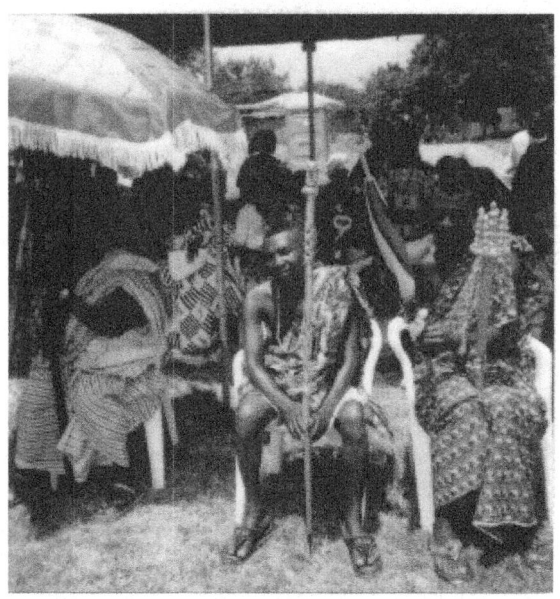

AMERICA

Dr. Nancy Franklin, Georgia

"Thank you God for answering my prayers by sending Your apostle to (the region) to unite the believers ... "

Prophetess Nancy Haney, Alaska

"God has never given me this before. I see circles and circles and circles ... you drink and you draw from one circle to the other, and that's what you do, you drink and draw and you bring these circles together ... Pulling many groups together. All these groups need each other ... He can use you for you have ears to hear and you hear His deep truth. You are filtering what is nonsense and what is real ... because you have been in that circle, and because of what you say they are going to merge. It is going to expand, become bigger than you could imagine."

Man of God (Georgia), Requesting to be Discipled while attending the coronation of a King in Africa, Georgia

"…at my age, it is hard to believe I am learning so much in these few days about what I did not know…realizing what it is to know that I know how it is to live within God's word each day. Will you consider discipling me?"

Pastor, Host of "Praise the Lord", TBN, "…**The fruit of the ministry is evident in your testimony…**"

International Prophet, "**You have remained steadfast to God's plan and God will continue to send you forth for His plan and purpose to be fulfilled, and for the thousands who have not knelt…**"

President, Christian Publishing Company

"**Only God could orchestrate such a grand plan…**"

Prayer Director, International Prayer Center

"God is opening many doors for you…"

Christian Publisher,

"God has given you a powerful voice and a sweet spirit…"

Pastor, Southern California

"God is raising you up and sending you forth to many nations…"

International Apostle

"God is doing a mighty work through you, for His righteousness precedes you, showers over you and follows you as a mighty wake. May it continue for each of your days…"

Prophetic Prayer Partner, Minnesota

"Only God could walk you through these days… accomplish so much through you, in the midst of your daily situations, the many blessings shared during each of your travels will continue to shower blessings upon each of the many households around the world…"

AUSTRALIA

Newcastle, New South Wales, Australia

Pastor Mark, "…**the staff and business leaders heard the message of Personal &Professional Life Management this week, so we are blessed you agreed to preach the word to our church this morning.**"

Prayer Team Meeting "**We know now how we will we be able to continue this mighty work when you are not in our midst…**"

Four Square Gospel Church, Aboriginal Cultural Center
Pastor Rex, "**God blessed us through your preaching on Easter Sunday. We will never forget that you were in our midst … God brought new people to**

Jesus today & we thank God for what He has done because you answered His call."

ENGLAND

London, England

Pastor Vincent, Glory House, East London,

"...the honor is ours this Easter Sunday."

Associate Pastor,

"The Glory of our God Almighty shines upon you and through you in your speaking and your actions...we give Him praise."

Protocol Team,

"God has mightily blessed us, by sending you into our midst."

Pastor Arnold,

"You have blessed the people of this congregation, and in His wisdom and timing, may He bring you back into our midst again, very soon."

Pastor, West London,

> **"We rejoice with you in hearing and seeing the mighty things God is doing."**

Pastor, South London, **"Our God is evidenced in your life and your speaking, while we continue to thank God for the work He is doing through you…"**

High Commissioner, Kingdom of Tonga, serving in the Embassy in London, England; Ambassador, Akosita, **"God's timing is always right…for you to be with us, prior to the Economic Summit, to meet and pray with us…"**

Sunderland, England

Anglican, Former Church of Pastor Smith Wigglesworth

Pastor Day, "**I thank God for sending you to our church this morning, for serving communion to me, and for renewing and restoring me for the call upon my life.**"

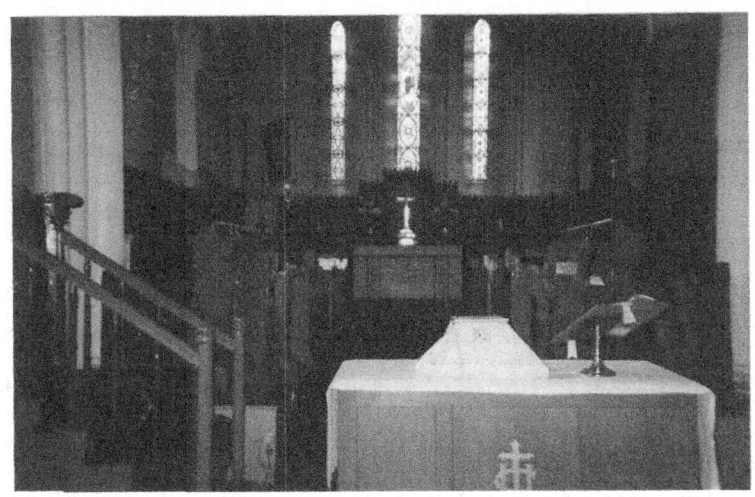

Kingdom of TONGA

Pastor Isileli Taukolo, "**Our board and business leaders were fasting and praying and God confirmed He was sending someone to us. We are deeply touched by the message God sent to us, through you.**"

Minister of Finance, Tasi, "**Our meeting was an answer to my prayers, and I thank you for providing the seminar for our senior staff members, and meeting with them individually for prayer and coaching.**"

Government Office, "**Thank you for speaking today and for staying and praying with us.**"

Interpreter, Sela

About the Author

The LORD fulfills upon His promises within the scriptures. He has equipped and trained her while He:

- Places her feet on the soil of every continent,
- Sends her forth without an extra coin or tunic,
- Arranges flights and accommodations in each nation,
- Introduces her before she arrives,
- Lifts her up and encourages her,
- Seats her before governors and kings,
- Fills her as an empty vessel,
- Shares His wisdom and word of knowledge,
- Blesses and heals the people in her path,
- Comforts and re-encourages her to encourage pastors, prophets, believers, teachers & evangelists,
- Touches people individually in conferences/multitude,
- Speaks through her with power and authority,
- Takes people into gift of laughter when she preaches,
- Addresses situations the body of Christ is facing,

- Unites the people in the region,
- Confirms His word through her with each prayer & message shared,
- Speaks through her so people hear His words in their own language, especially when the translators also experience the gift of laughter and stop translating.
- Directs her path to <u>speak life</u> into each situation whether God sends people to her to be re-encouraged or he asks her to pray with a pastor, the church, or someone in a store or a restaurant, etc.

God has taken Sheila around the globe, church to church, business to business, nation to nation.

Many confirm she walks in the five-fold ministry. She does not use a title because God does the work while He sends her as an apostle and prophet while He orchestrates all arrangements for her to preach, teach, and evangelize.

People attending the conferences often say her segments are like watching someone walk out of the bible, share for a while and then, go right back in the bible, aka continue upon her journey in HIStory.

Email: hisbest4usorders@gmail.com
Use the Subject Line: ***It's A Faith Walk!***

Web site: http://hisbest4us.org

Facebook HISBest4us

Dare To Believe, Then Command

Smith Wigglesworth – 1919

"Verily, verily, I say unto you; He that believeth on Me, the works that I do shall he do also: and greater works than these shall he do; because I go unto My Father. And whatsoever ye shall ask in My name, that will I do, that the Father may be glorified in the Son. If ye shall ask any thing in My name, I will do it." John 14:12-14.

Jesus is speaking here, and the Spirit of God can take these words of His and make them real to us. "He that believeth on Me... greater works than these shall he do." What a word! Is it true? If you want the truth, where will you get it? "Thy word is truth," Christ said to the Father. When you take up God's Word you get the truth. God is not the author of confusion or error, but He sends forth His light and truth to lead us into His holy habitation, where we receive a revelation of the truth like unto the noon day in all its clearness.

The Word of God works effectually in us as we believe it. It changes us and brings us into new fellowship with the Father, with the Son, and with the Holy Spirit, into a holy communion, into an unwavering faith, into a mighty assurance, and it will make us partakers of the very nature and likeness of God as we receive His great and exceeding precious promises and believe them. Faith comet by hearing, and hearing by the Word of God. Faith is the operative power.

We read that Christ opened the understanding of His disciples, and He will open up our understanding and our hearts and will show us wonderful things that we should never know but for the mighty revelation and enlightenment of the Spirit that He gives to us.

I do not know of any greater words than those found in Romans 4:16, "Therefore it is of faith, that it might be by grace." Grace is God's benediction coming right down to you, and when you open the door to Him—that is an act of faith—He does all you want and will fulfill all your desires. "It is of faith, that it might be by grace." You open the way for God to work as you believe His Word, and God will come in and supply your every need all along the way.

Our Lord Jesus said to His disciples and He says to us in this passage in the 14th of John, "You have seen Me work and you know how I work. You shall do the very same things that I am doing, and greater things shall you do, because I am going to the Father, and as you make petition in My name I will work. I will do what you ask, and by this the Father shall be glorified."

Did any one ever work as He did? I do not mean His carpentering. I refer to His work in the hearts of the people. He drew them to Him. They came with their needs, with their sicknesses, with their oppression, and He relieved them all. This royal Visitor, who came from the Father to express His love, talked to men, spent time with them in their homes, found out their every need. He went about doing good and healing all who were oppressed of the devil, and He said to them and He says to us, "You see what I have been doing, healing the sick, relieving the oppressed, casting out demons. The works that I do shall ye do also." Dare you believe? Will you take up the work that He left and carry it on?

"He that believeth on Me!" What is this? What does it mean? How can just believing bring these things to pass? What virtue is there in it? There is virtue in these words because He declares them. If we will receive this word and declare it, the greater works shall be accomplished. This is a positive declaration of His, "He that believeth on Me, greater works than these shall he do," but unbelief has hindered our progress in the realm of the spiritual.

Put away unbelief. Open your heart to God's grace. Then God will come in and place in you a definite faith. He wants to remove every obstruction that is in the world before you. By His grace He will enable you to be so established in His truth, so strong in the Lord and in the power of His might, that whatever comes across your path to obstruct you, you can arise in divine power and rebuke and destroy it.

It is a matter of definite and clear understanding between us and God. To recognize that Christ has a life force to put into us, changes everything that we dare to *believe* it will change. He that believes that Jesus is the Christ overcomes the world. Because we believe that Jesus is the Christ, the essence of divine life is in us by faith and causes a perfect separation between us and the world. We have no room for sin. It is a joyful thing for us to be doing that which is right. He will cause that abundance of grace to so flow into our hearts that sin shall not have dominion over us. Sin shall not have dominion; nor sickness, nor affliction. "He that believeth"—he that dares to believe—he that dares to trust—will see victory over every oppression of the enemy.

A needy creature came to me in a meeting, all withered and wasted. He had no hope. There was absolute death in his eyes. He was so helpless he had to have some one on each side to bear him up. He came to me and said in a whisper, "Can you help me?" Will Jesus answer? "He that believeth on Me, the works that I do shall he do also; and greater works than these.... Behold, I give you power... over all the power of the enemy." These are the words of our Lord Jesus. It is not our word but the word of the Lord, and as this word is in us He can make it like a burning passion in us. We make the Word of God as we believe it our own. We receive the Word and we have the very life of Christ in us. We become supernatural by the power of God. We find this power working through every part of our being.

Now Christ gives us something besides faith. He gives us something to make faith effectual. Whatsoever you desire, if you believe in your heart you shall have. Christ said, "Have faith in God. For verily I say unto you, That whosoever shall say unto this mountain, Be thou removed, and be thou cast into the sea; and shall not doubt in his heart, but shall believe that those things which he saith shall come to pass; he shall have whatsoever he saith. Therefore I say unto you, What things soever ye desire, when ye pray, believe that ye receive them, and ye shall have them." Mark 11:22-24. Whatsoever he saith! Dare to say in faith and it shall be done. These things have been promised by Christ and He does not lie.

This afflicted man stood before me helpless and withered. He had had cancer in his stomach. The physicians had operated upon him to take away the cancer from the stomach, but complications had arisen with the result that no food could enter the man's stomach. He could not swallow anything. So in order to keep him alive they made a hole in his stomach and put in a tube about nine inches long with a cup at the top, and he was fed with liquid through this tube. For three months he had been just kept alive but was like a skeleton.

What was I to say to him? "If thou wouldest believe, thou shouldest see the glory of God."

Here was the word of Christ, "He that believeth on me, the works that I do shall he do also, and greater works than these shall he do; because I go unto My Father." The Word of God is truth. Christ is with the Father and grants us our requests, and makes these things manifest, if we believe. What should I do in the presence of a case like this? "Believe the Word." So I believed the Word which says, "He shall have whatsoever he saith." Mark 11:23. I said, "Go home, and have a good supper." He said, "I cannot swallow."

"Go home, and have a good supper," I repeated. "On the authority of the Word of God I say it. Christ says that he that believes that these things which he says shall come to pass he shall have whatsoever he says. So I say, Go home in the name of Jesus, and have a good supper."

He went home. Supper was prepared. Many times he had had food in his mouth but had always been forced to spit it out again. But I dared to believe that he would be able to swallow that night. So that man filled his mouth full as he had done before, and because some one dared to believe God's Word and said to him, "You shall have a good supper in the name of Jesus," when he chewed his food it went down in the normal way into his stomach, and he ate until he was quite satisfied.

He and his family went to bed filled with joy. The next morning when they arose they were filled with the same joy. Life had begun again. Naturally he looked down to see the hole that had been made in his stomach by the physicians. But God knew that he did not want two holes, and so when God opened the normal passage He closed the other hole in his stomach. This is the kind of God we have all the time, a God who knows, a God who acts, and brings things to pass when we believe. Dare to believe, and then dare to speak and you shall have whatsoever you say if you doubt not.

A woman came to me one night and inquired, "Can I hear again? Is it possible for me to hear again? I have had several operations and the drums of my ears have been taken away." I said, "If God has not forgotten how to make drums for ears you can hear again." Do you think God has forgotten? What does God forget? He forgets our sins, when we are forgiven, but He has not forgotten how to make drums for ears.

Not long ago the power of God was very much upon a meeting that I was holding. I was telling the people that they could be healed without my going to them. If they would rise up I would pray and the Lord would heal. There was a man who put up his hand. I said, "Cannot that man rise?" The folks near him said he could not, and lifted him hp. The Lord healed him the ribs that were broken were knit together again and were healed.

There was such faith in the place that a little girl cried out, "Please, gentleman, come to me." You could not see her, she was so small. The mother said, "My little girl wants you to come." So I went down there to this child, who although fourteen years of age was very small. She said with tears streaming down her face, "Will you pray for me?" I said, "Dare you believe?" She said, "O yes." I prayed and placed my hands on her head in the name of Jesus.

"Mother," she said, "I am being healed. Take these things off— take them all off." The mother loosed straps and bands and then the child said, "Mother, I am sure I am healed. Take these off." She had straps on her legs and an iron on her foot about 3½ inches deep. She asked her mother to unstrap her. Her mother took off the straps. There were not many people with dry eyes as they saw that girl walk about with legs just as normal as when she was born. God healed her right away. What did it? She had cried, "Please, gentleman, come to me," and her longing was coupled with faith. May the Lord help us to be just like a simple child.

God has hidden these things from the wise and prudent, but He reveals them to babes. There is something in childlike faith in God that makes us dare to believe, and then to act. Whatever there is in your life that is bound, the name of Jesus and the power of that name will break it if you will only believe. Christ says, "If ye shall ask any thing in My name, I will do it." God will be glorified in Christ when you receive the overflowing life that comes from Christ in response to your faith.

Dare to believe. Do you think that truth is put into the Word to mock you? Don't you see that God really means that you should live in the world to relieve the oppression of the world? God answers us that we shall be quickened, be molded afresh, that the Word of God shall change everything that needs to be changed, both in us and in others, as we dare to believe and as we command things to be done. "Whosoever shall say unto this mountain, Be thou removed, and be thou cast into the sea; and shall not doubt in his heart, but shall believe that those things which he saith shall come to pass, he shall have whatsoever he saith."

Published in the Pentecostal Evangel on March 30, 1940

America was Founded upon Faith as the Path to Freedom and Liberty

Faith Monument[12]

On the main pedestal stands the heroic figure of "Faith" with her right hand pointing toward heaven and her left hand clutching the Bible. Upon the four buttresses also are seated figures emblematical of the principles upon which the Pilgrims founded their Commonwealth, each having a symbol referring to the Bible that "Faith" possesses; counter-clockwise from the feet of "Faith" are Morality, Law, Education, and Liberty. Each was carved from a solid block of granite, posed in the sitting position upon chairs with a high relief on either side of minor characteristics. Under "Morality" stand "Prophet" and "Evangelist"; under "Law" stand "Justice" and "Mercy"; under "Education" are "Youth" and "Wisdom"; and under "Liberty" stand "Tyranny Overthrown" and "Peace". On the face of the buttresses, beneath these figures are high reliefs in marble, representing scenes from Pilgrim history. Under "Morality" is "Embarcation"; under "Law" is "Treaty"; under "Education" is "Compact"; and under "Freedom" is "Landing". Upon the four faces of the main pedestal are large panels for records. The front panel is inscribed as follows: **"National Monument to the Forefathers: Erected by a grateful people in remembrance of their labors, sacrifices and sufferings for the cause of civil and religious liberty."** The right and left panels contain the names of those who came over in the *Mayflower.*

The rear panel, which was not engraved until recently, contains a quote from Governor William Bradford's famous history, ***Of Plymouth Plantation***:

"Thus out of small beginnings greater things have been produced by His hand that made all things of nothing and gives being to all things that are; and as one small candle may light a thousand, so the light here kindled hath shone unto many, yea in some sort to our whole nation; let the glorious name of Jehovah have all praise."

Made in the USA
Monee, IL
30 April 2022